Any Scapes to Color or Paint

I0483522

AUTHOR's NOTE

This book was inspired by my dad, Peter John Pukas...

He is always sketching and painting scenes with mountains, water, cabins,

trees (he loves trees) and rocks and flowers.

When I started this Adult Coloring Book adventure, it was just for fun but now

I am having more adventures in making them a Teaching Tool for Newbie Artists...

My intention is to capture trees, leaves, branches, foothills, mountains, rocks, sunsets and sunrises, moonlit nights and sunny days; the shape and curve of rocks, the way flowers and trees bend in the wind, to show the line of architecture in buildings and bridges and to show distance in the hills, sea, mountains, roads...

To use the wonderful photos (Public Domain Images-FREE) that people have taken and turn them into art tools for those of us that do not know how to perhaps sketch, paint or even haven't colored in years!

So pick up your crayons, pencil crayons, water colors, pastels or a paint brush

and just have some fun!

Who knows...it could be as RELAXING as everyone says it is!

Try it...You Might Like It ☺

Hugs N Ta,

Leesa Pukas-Salviulo

CAUTION...MAY CAUSE:
*Relaxation
*Stress Relief
*Artistic and Color Therapeutic Feelings
*JUST PLAIN HAPPINESS!!!
PLEASE USE YOUR COLORING PENCILS CAREFULLY!
ENJOY :)

Author: Leesa M Pukas-Salviulo
Publisher: Amazon.ca
Date Published:
Created with Public Domain Images
ISBN-13:
978-1530938544

ISBN-10:
1530938546

First edition

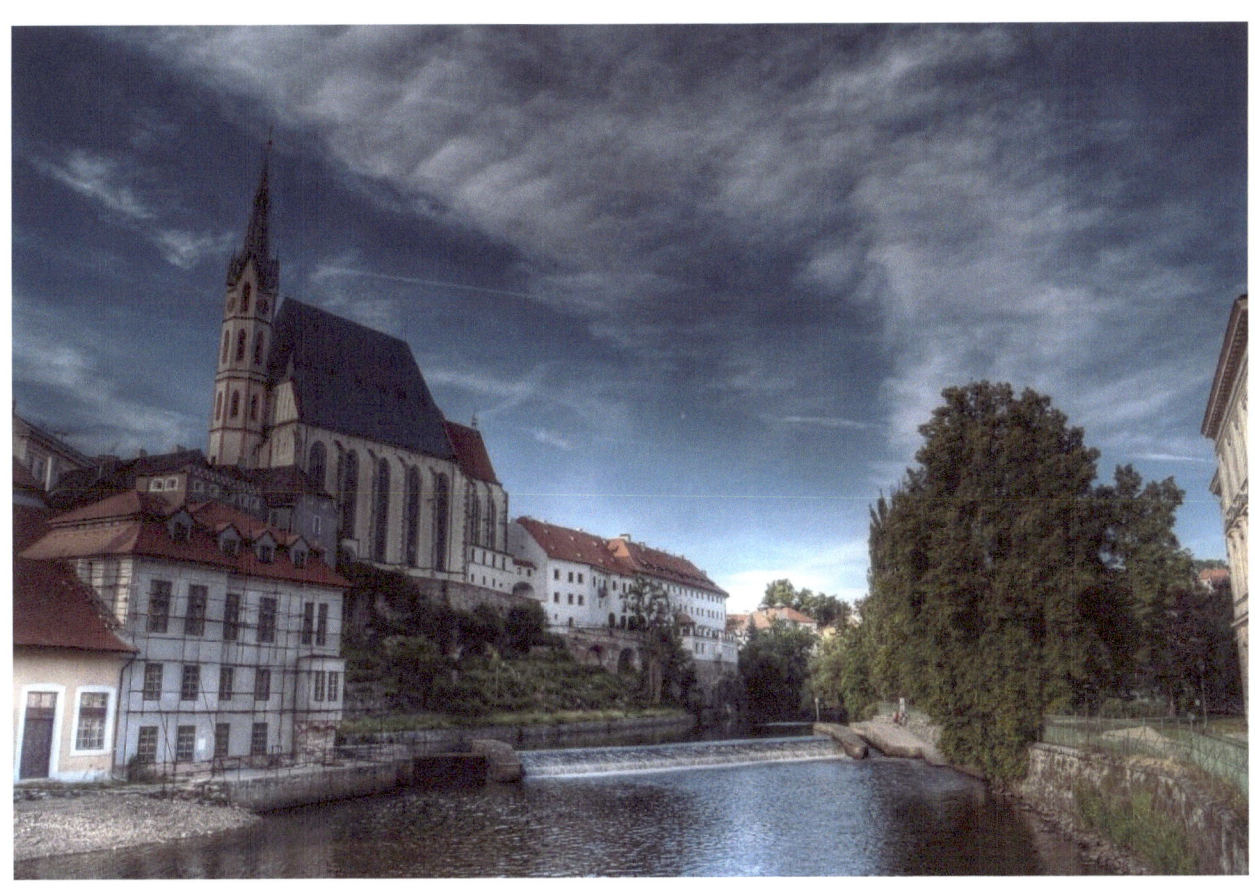

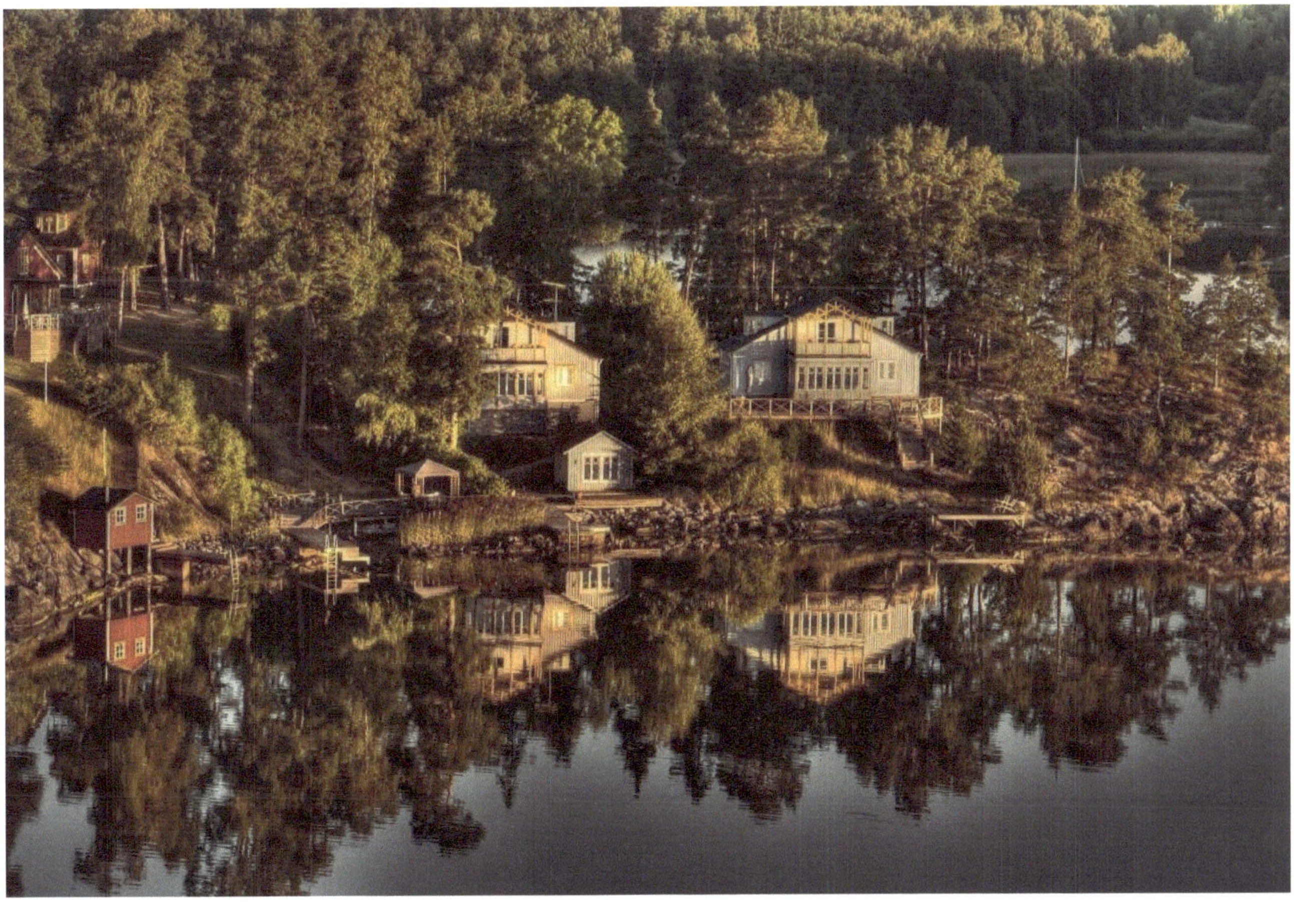

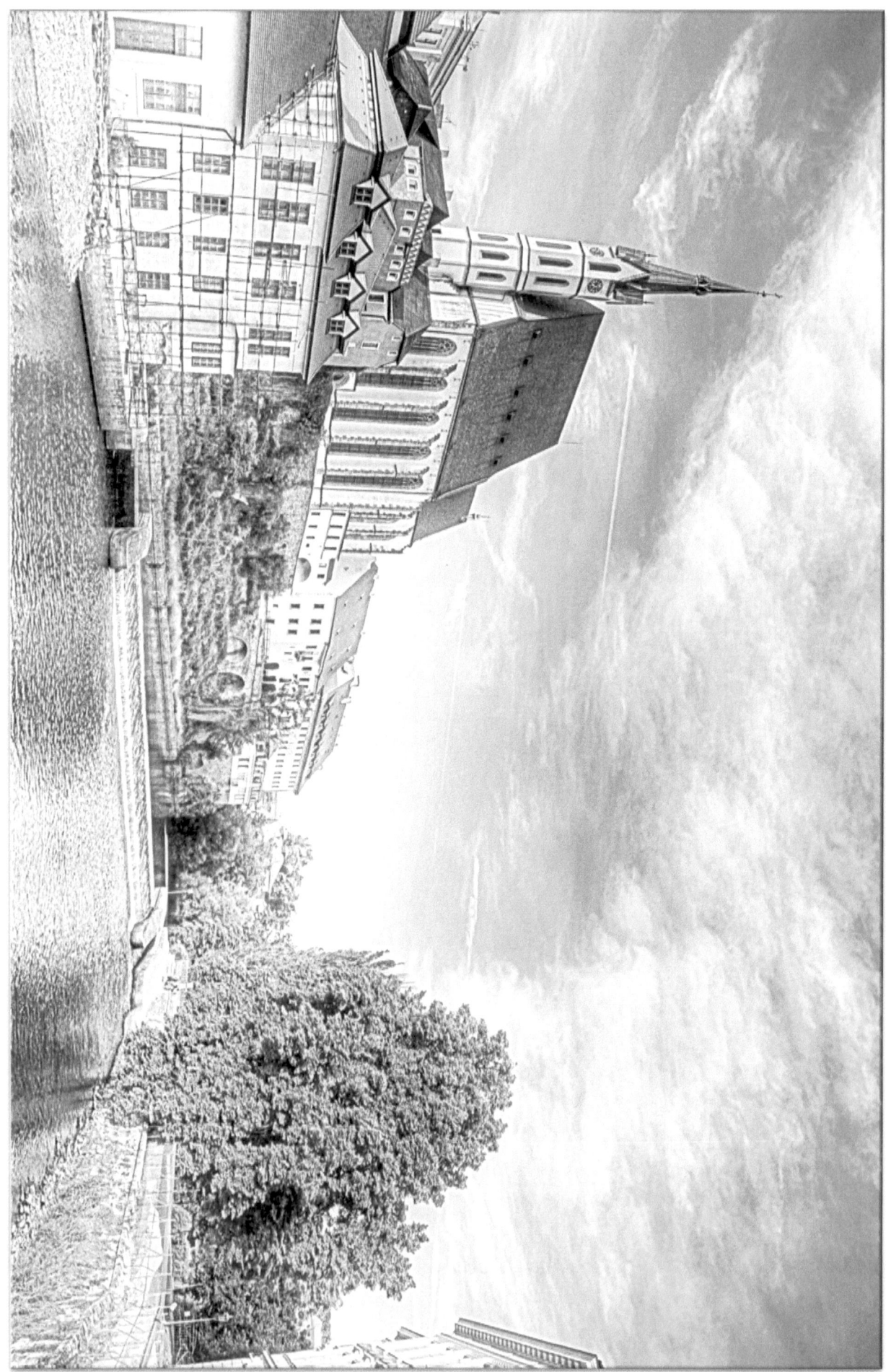

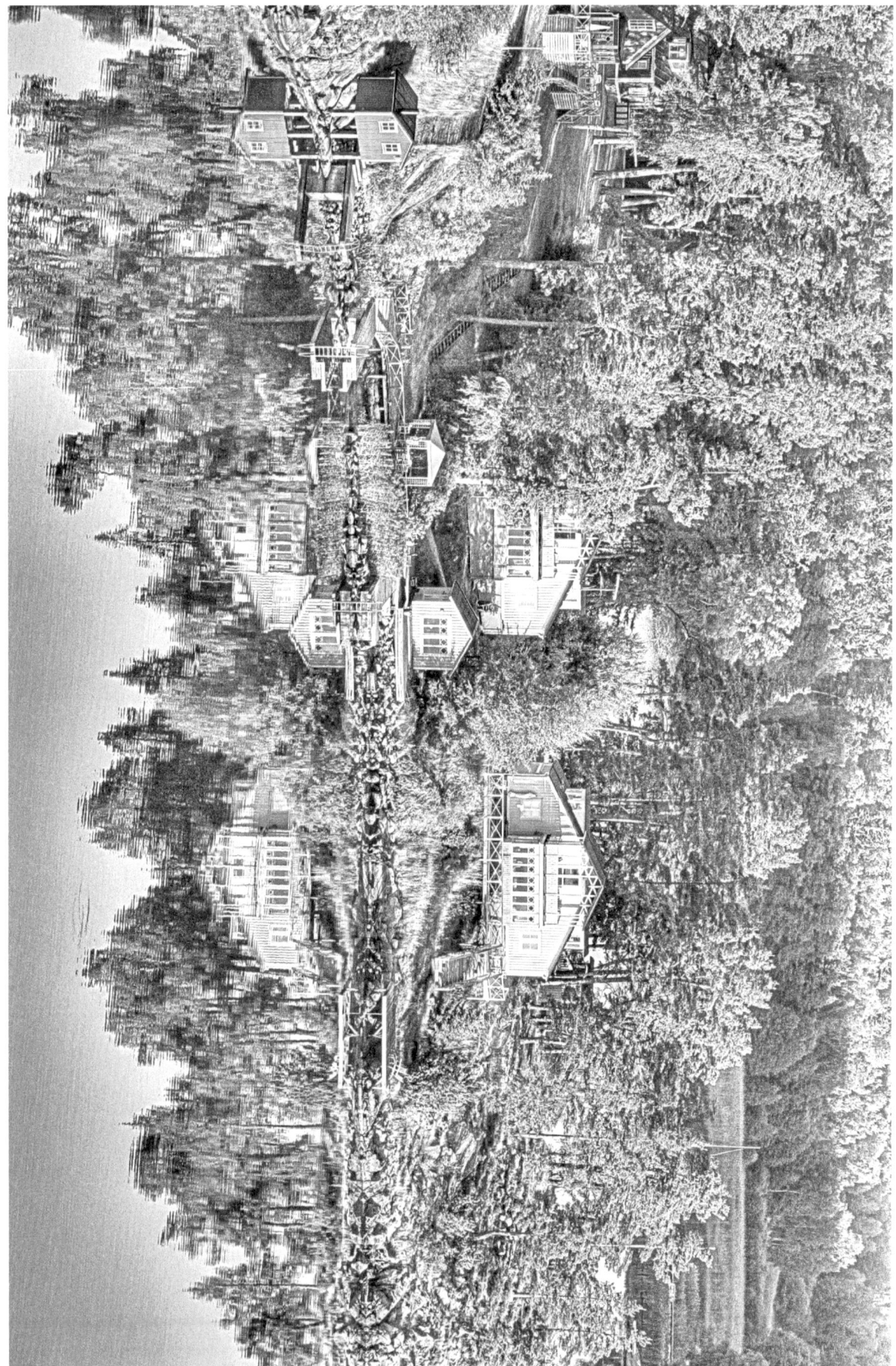

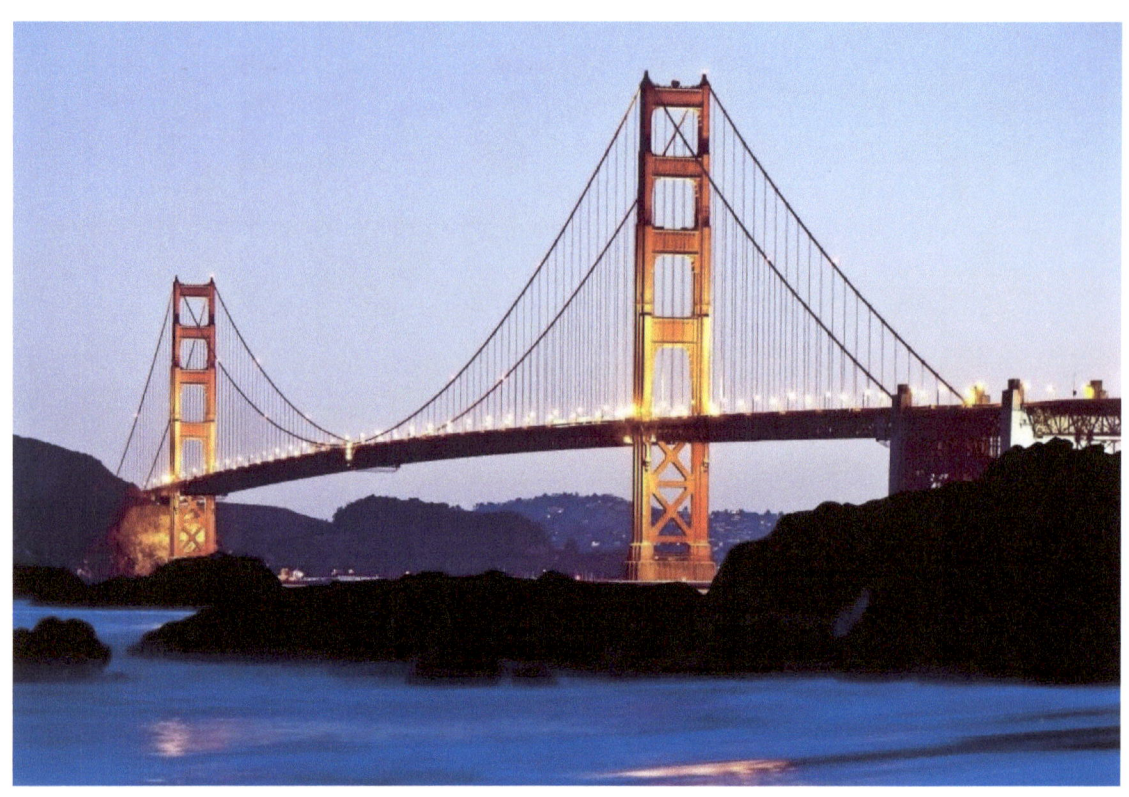

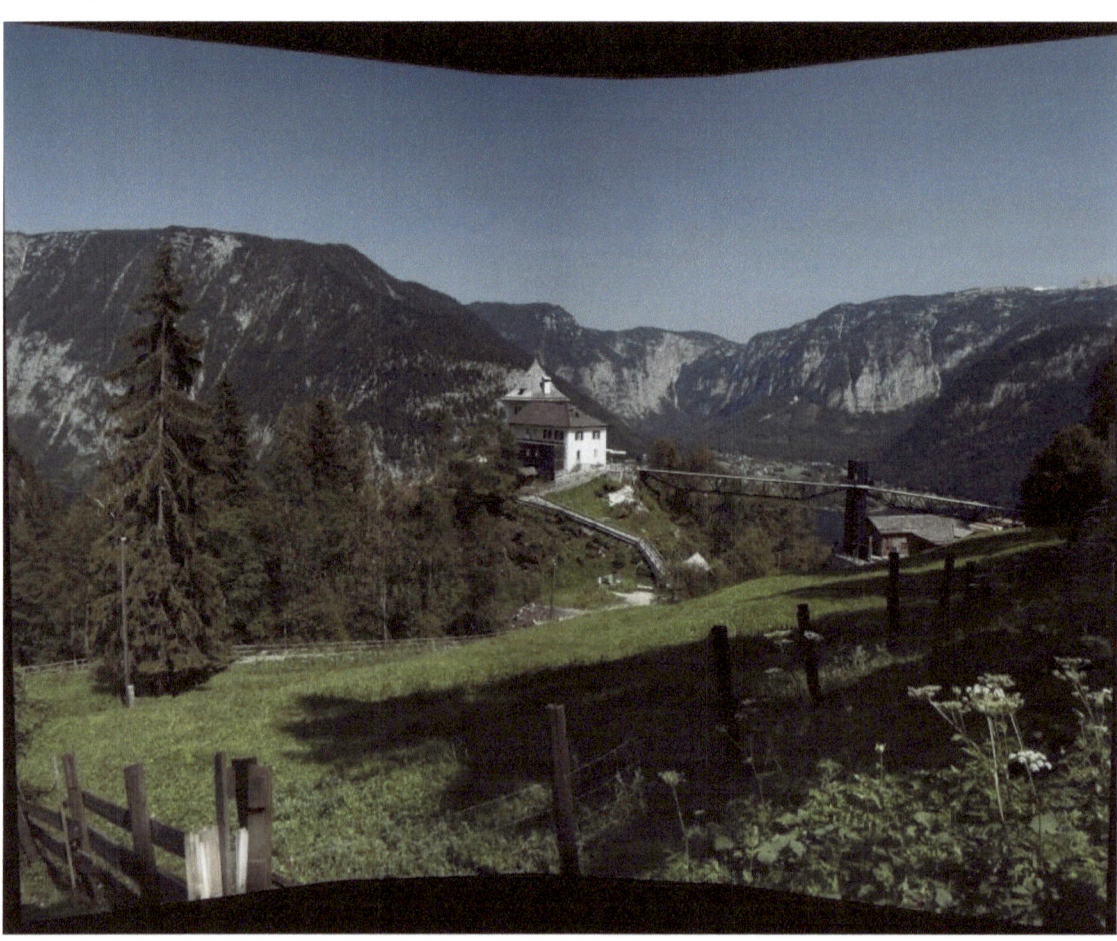

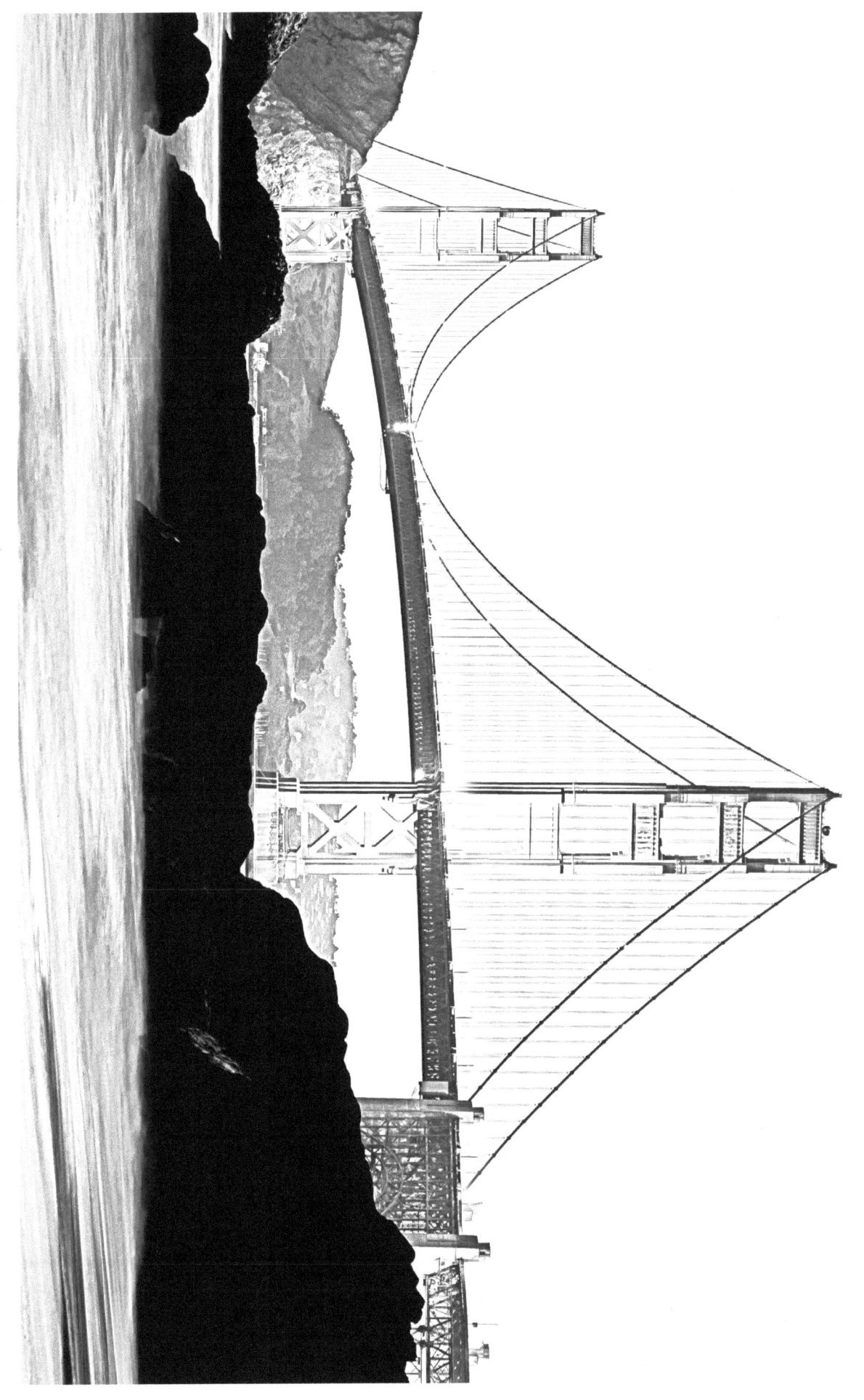

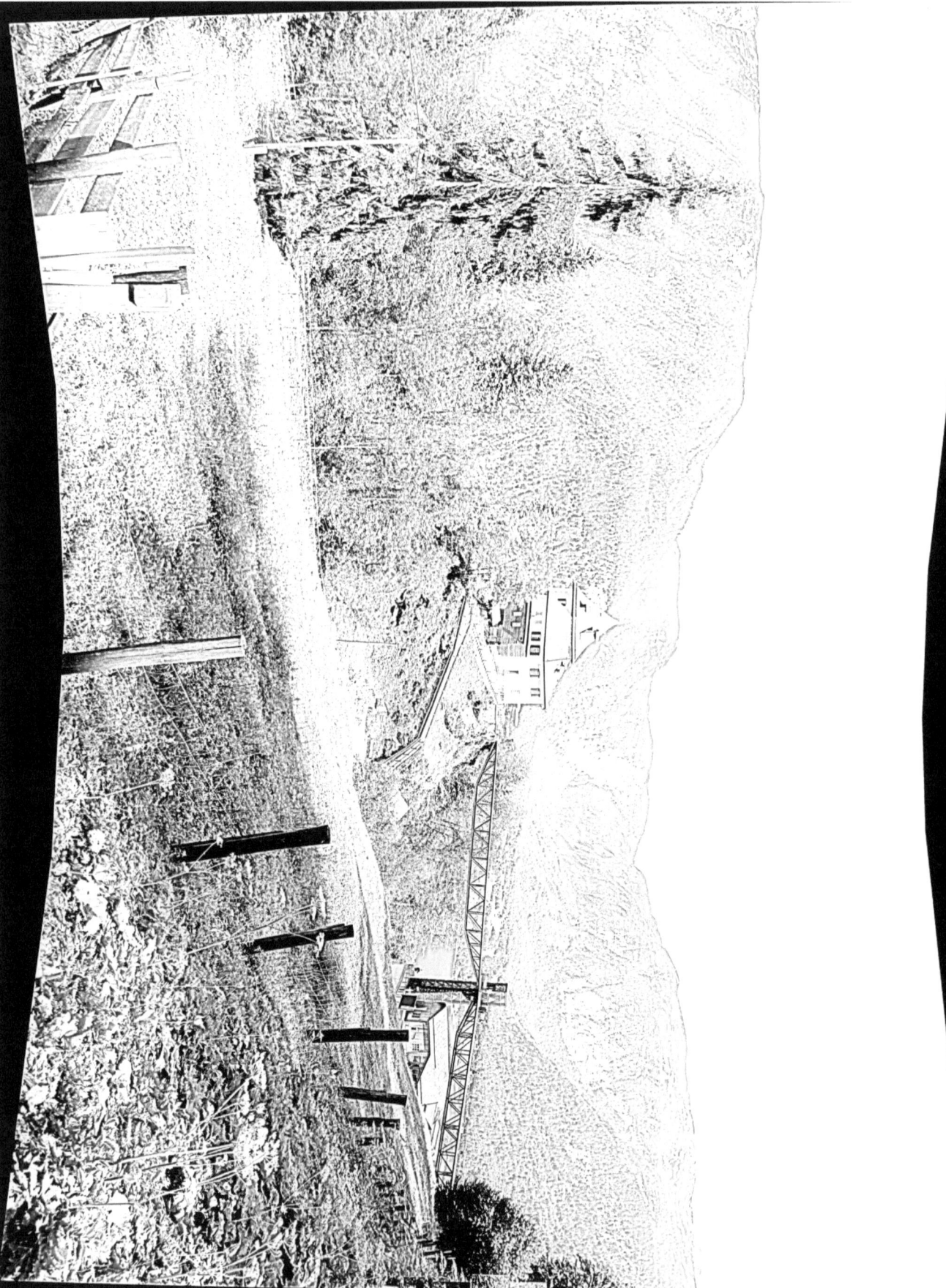

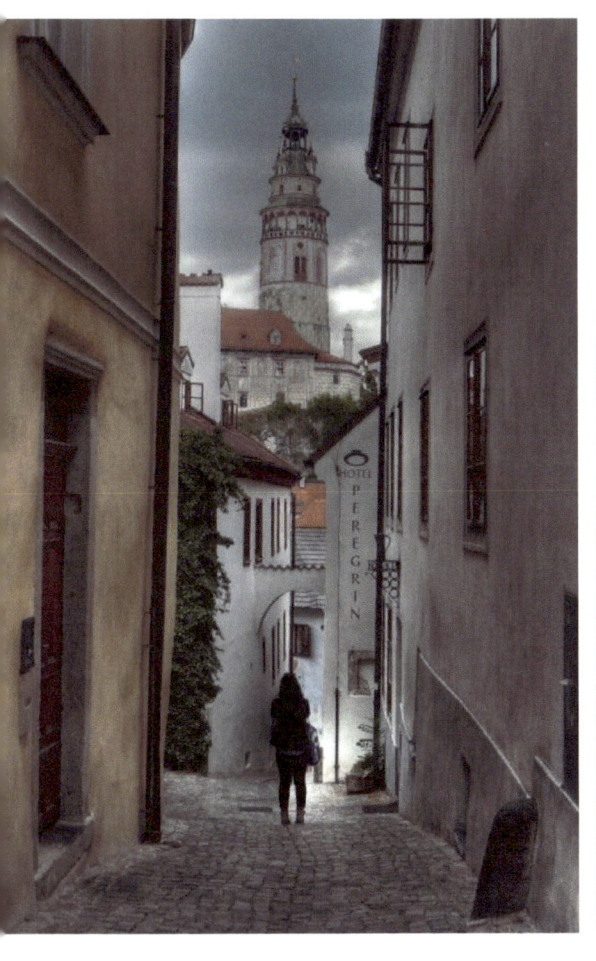

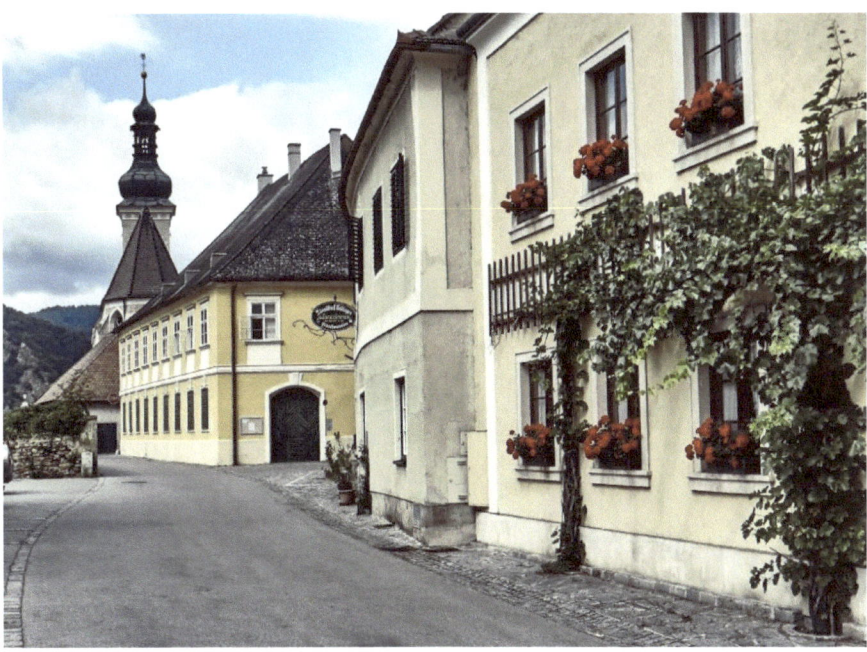

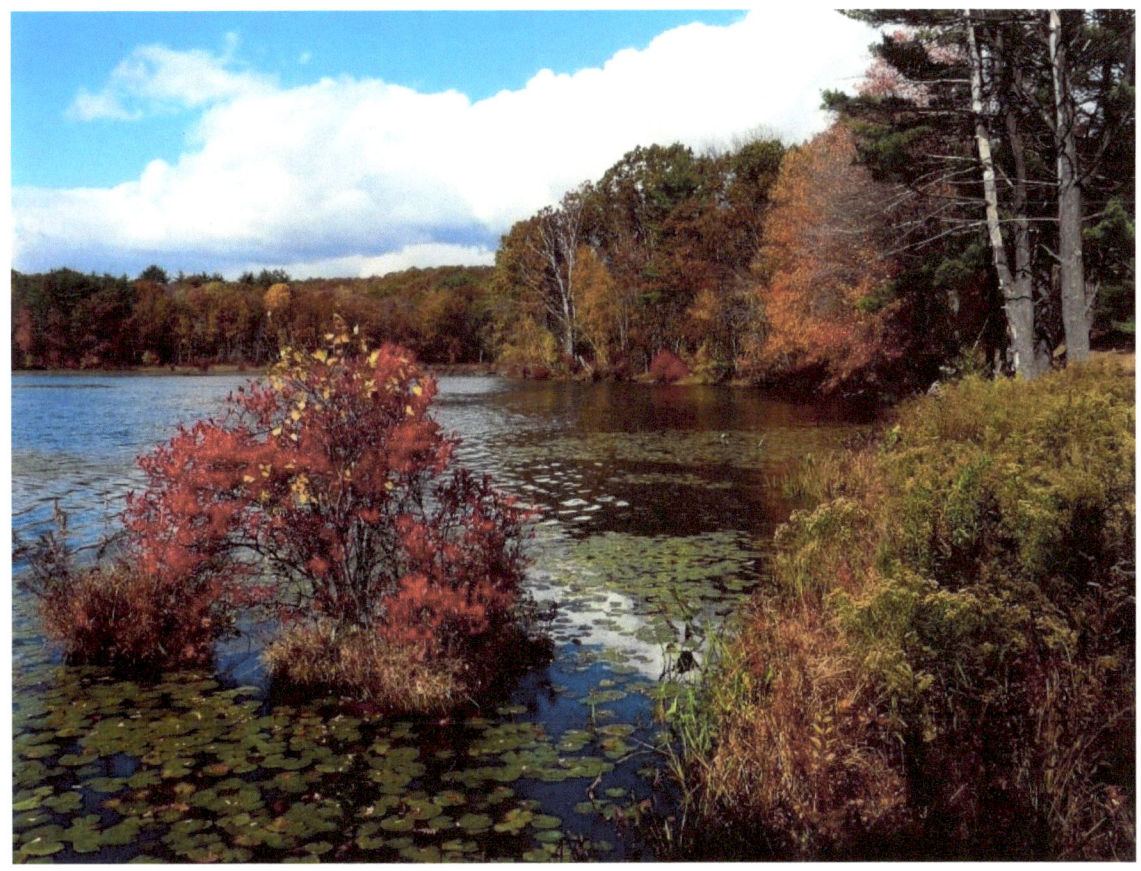

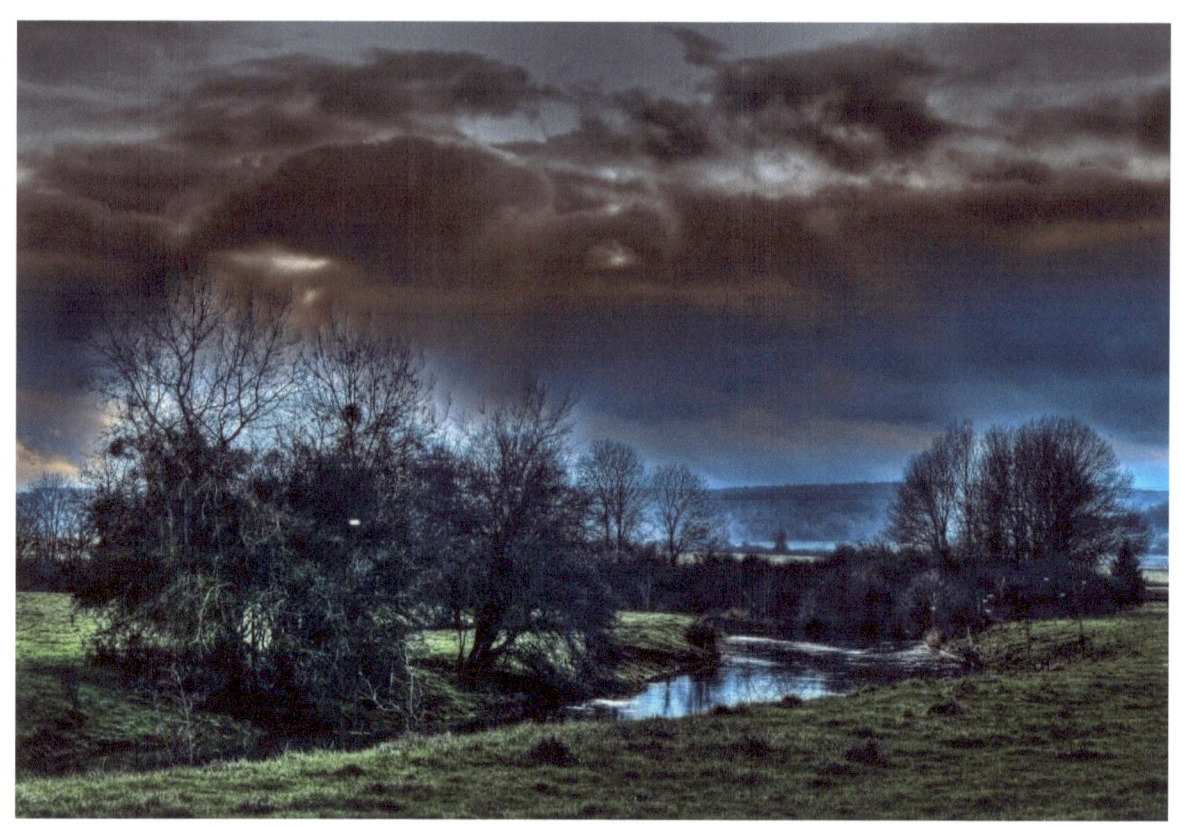

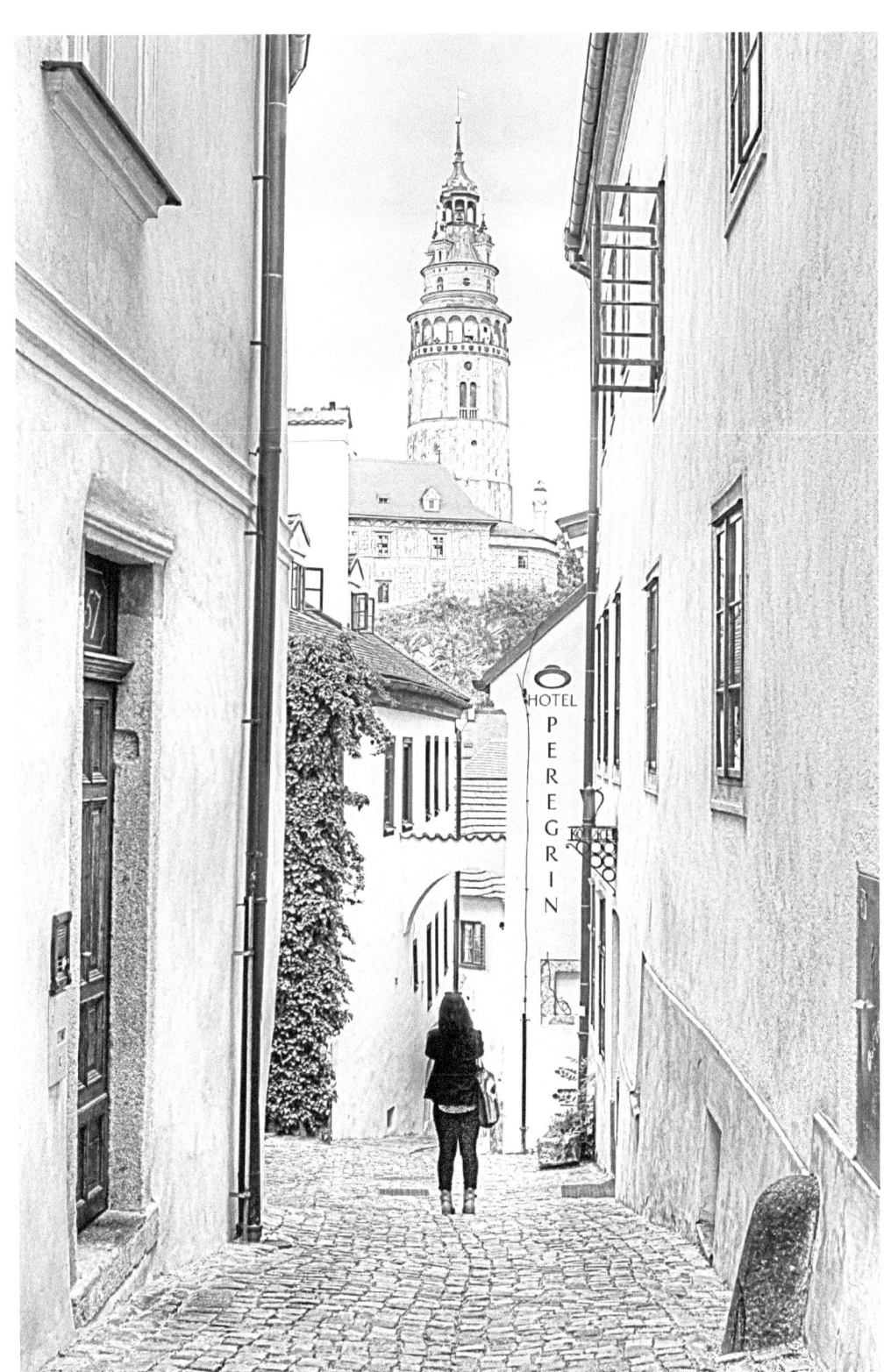

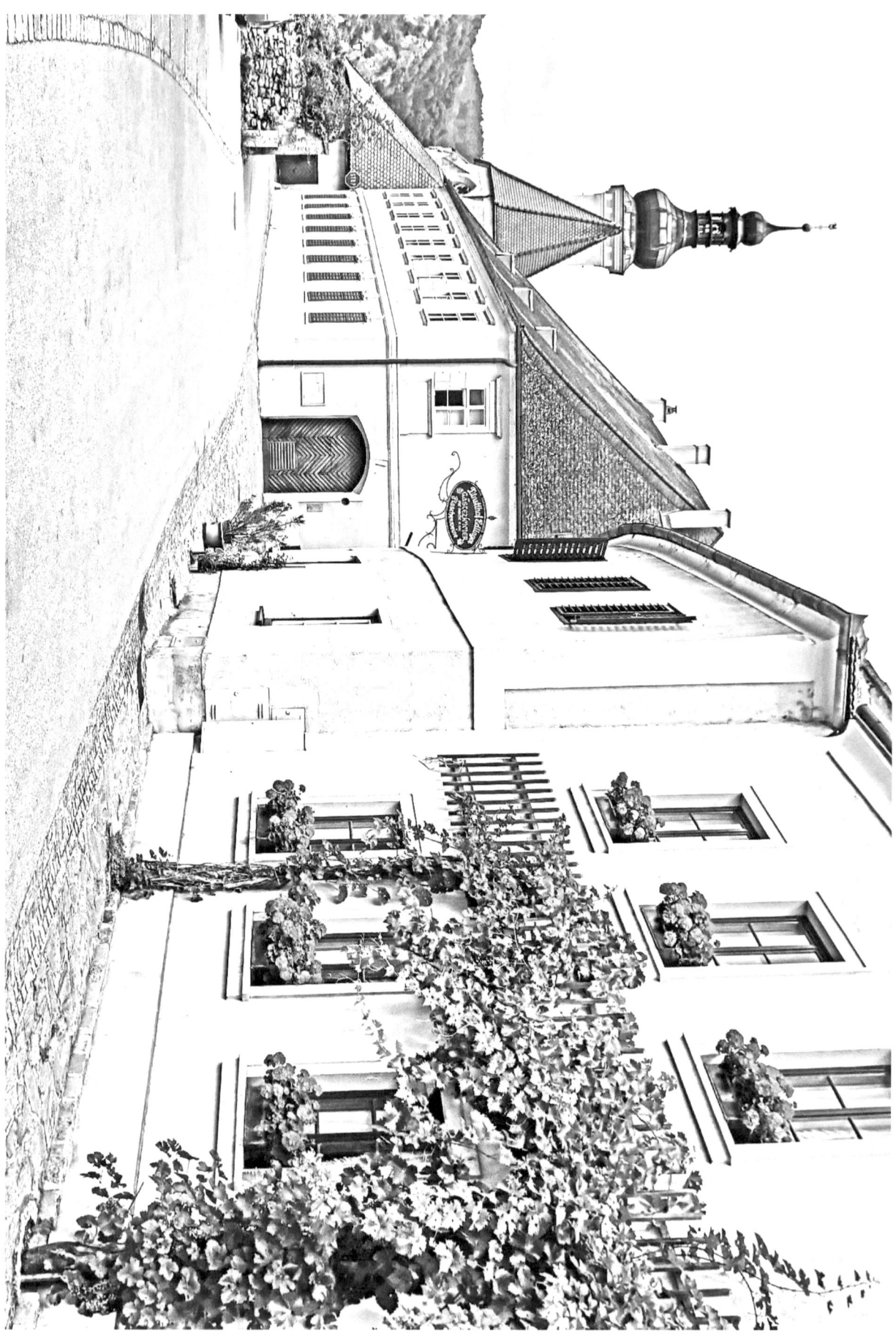

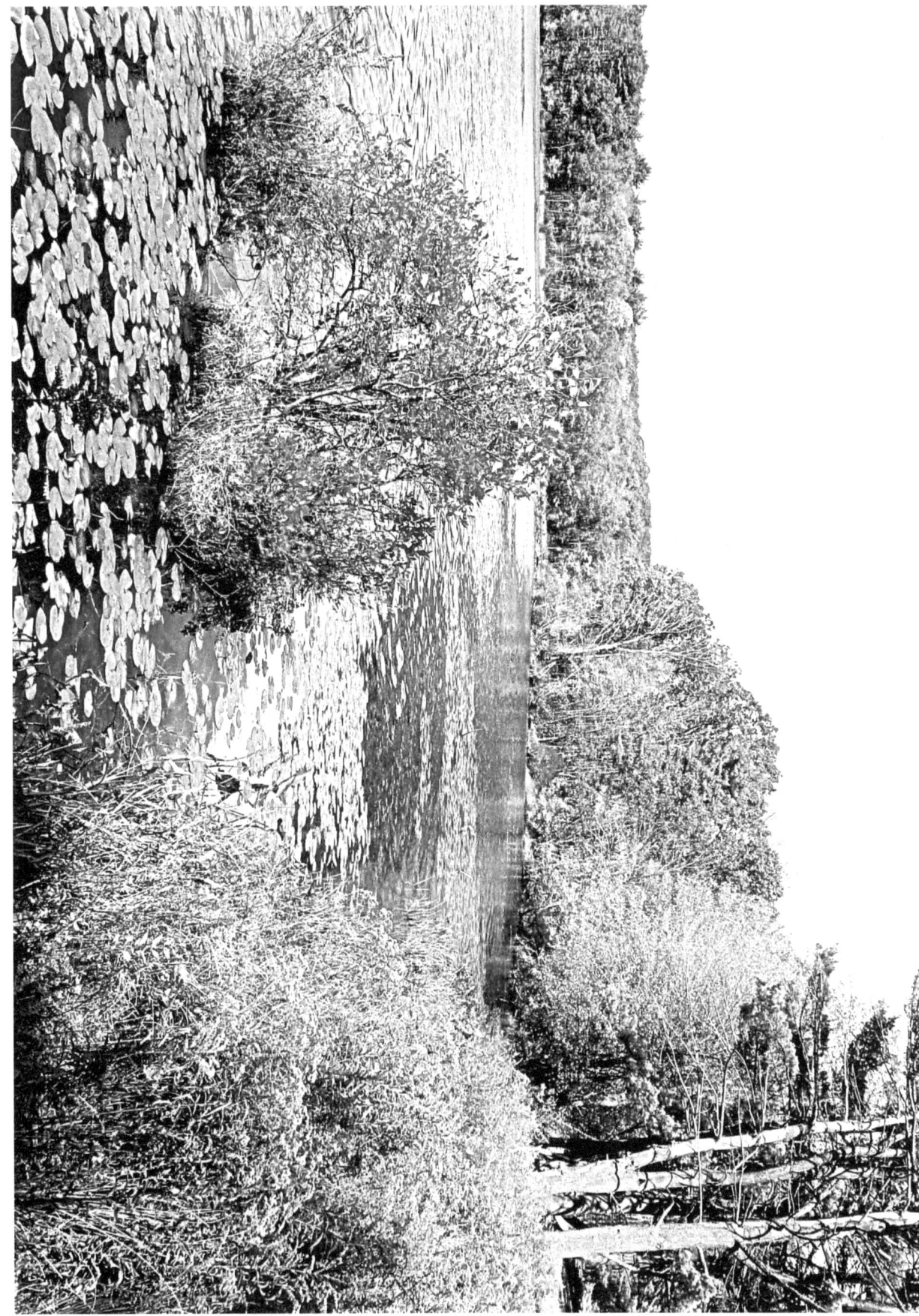

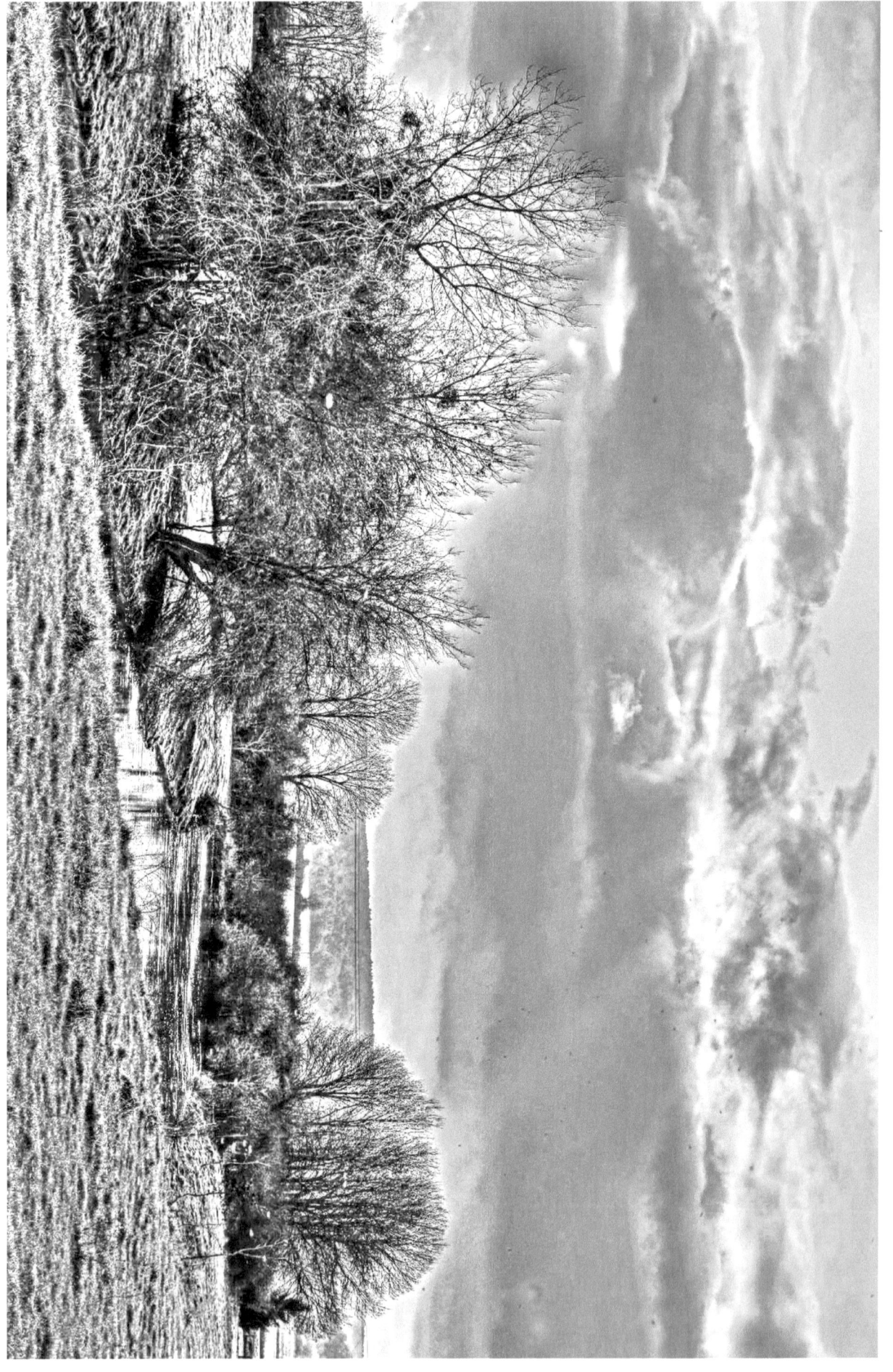

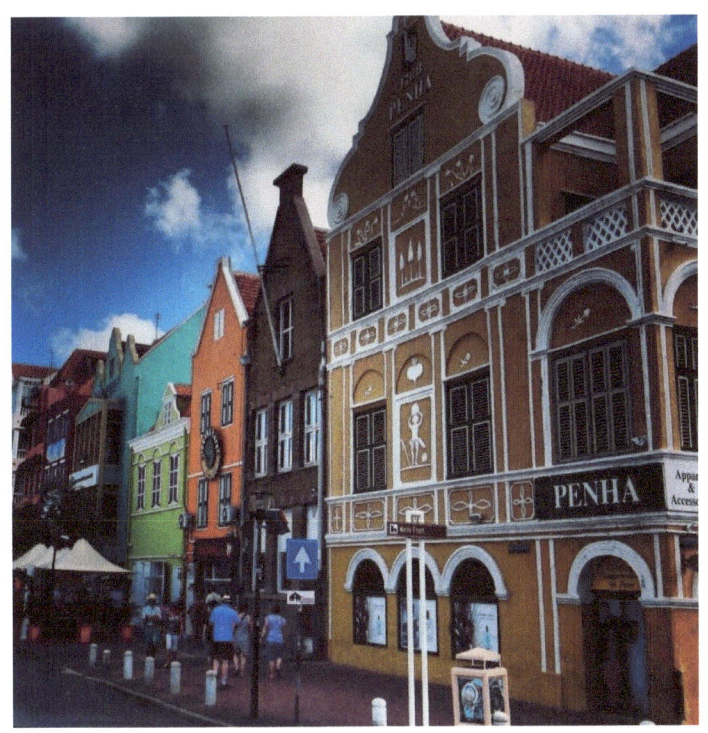

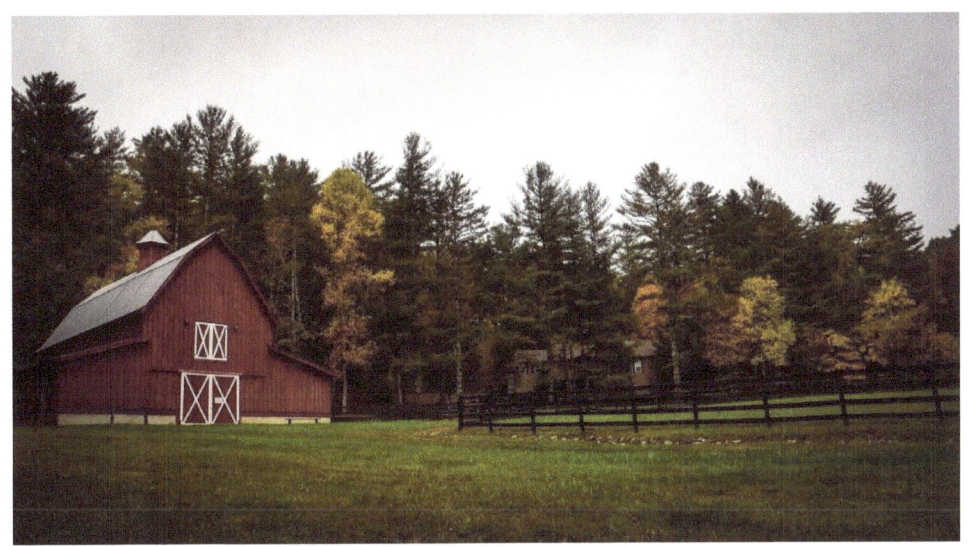

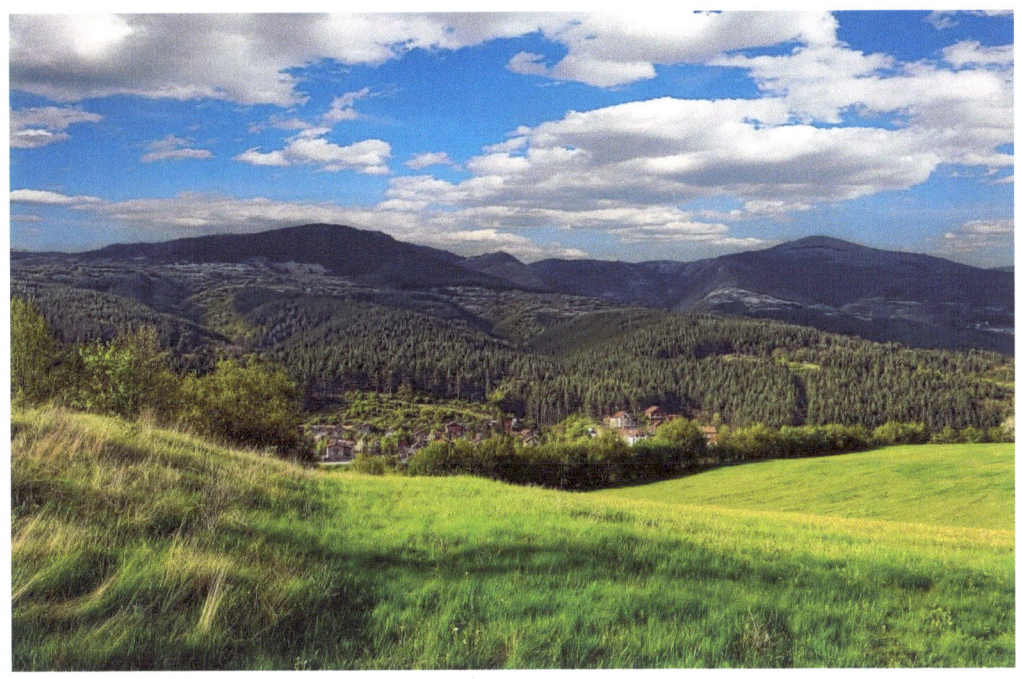

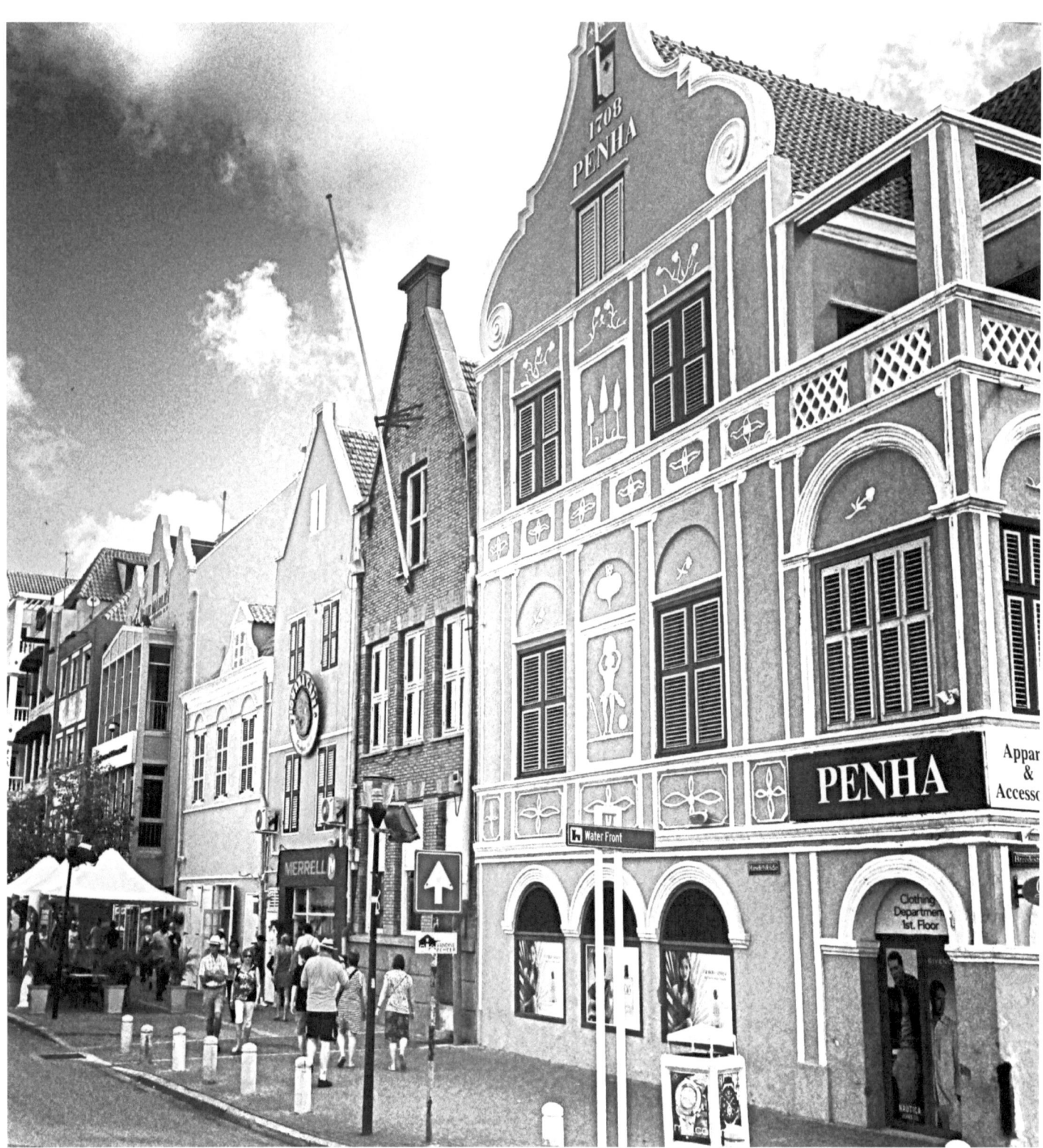

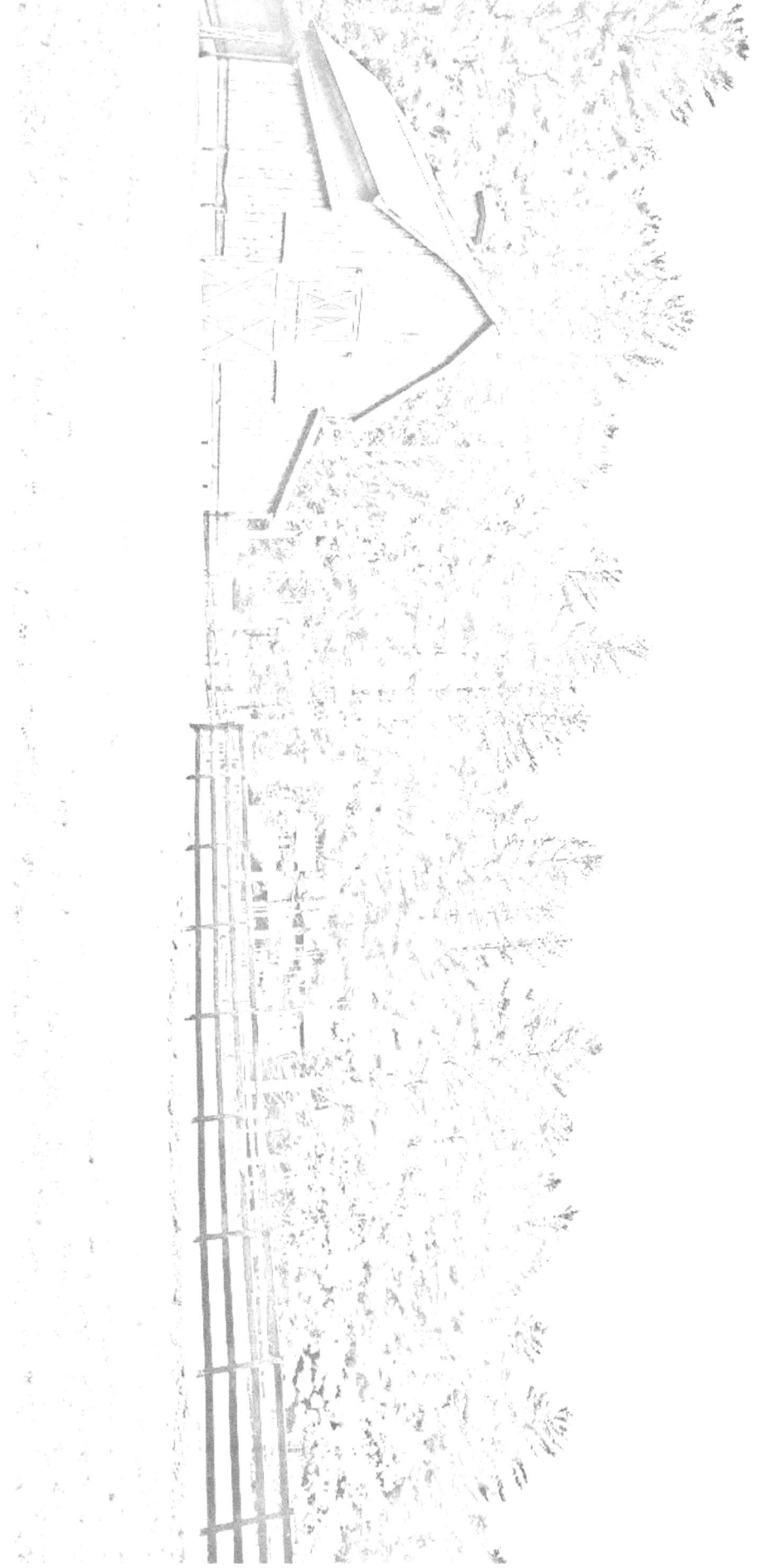

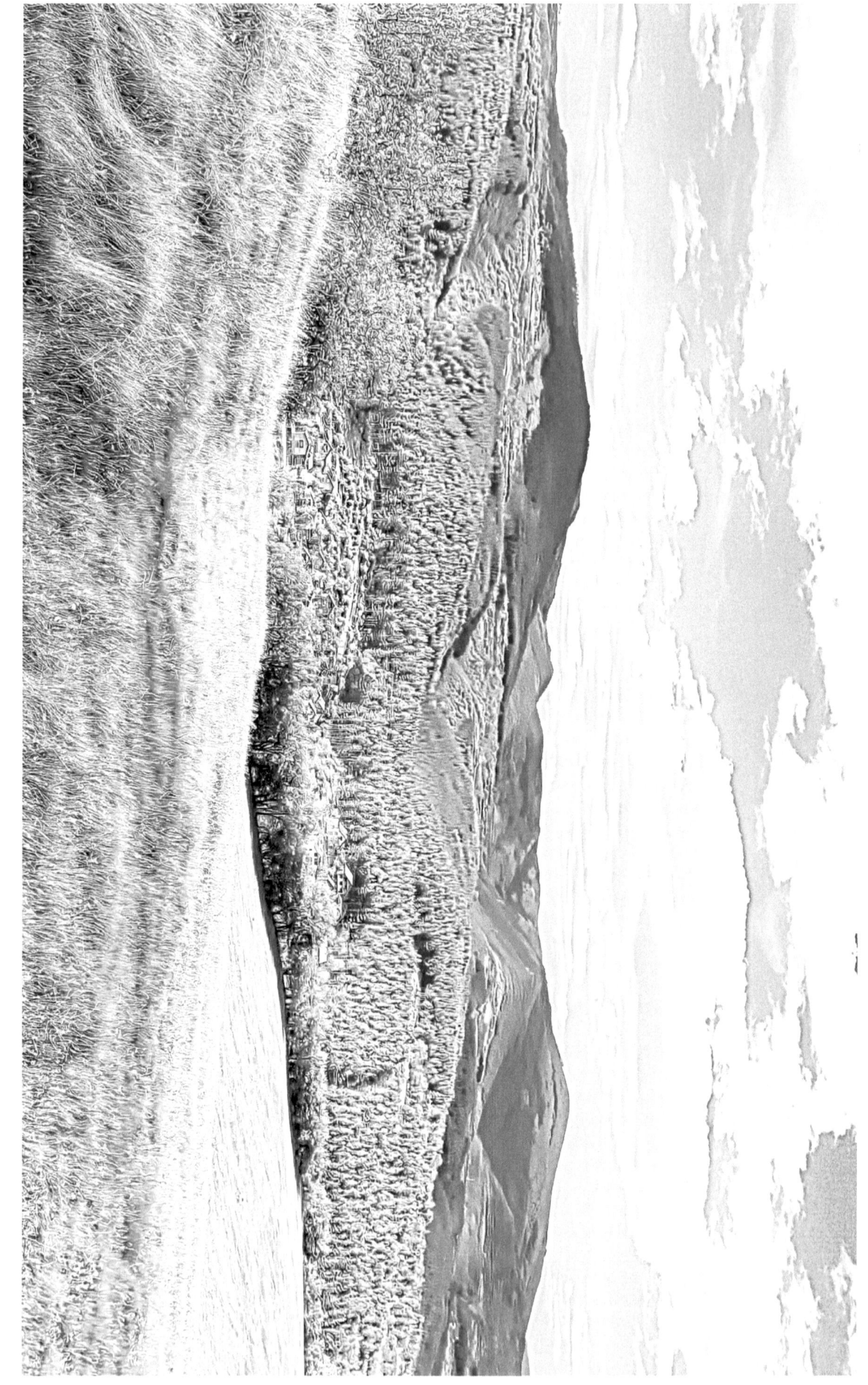

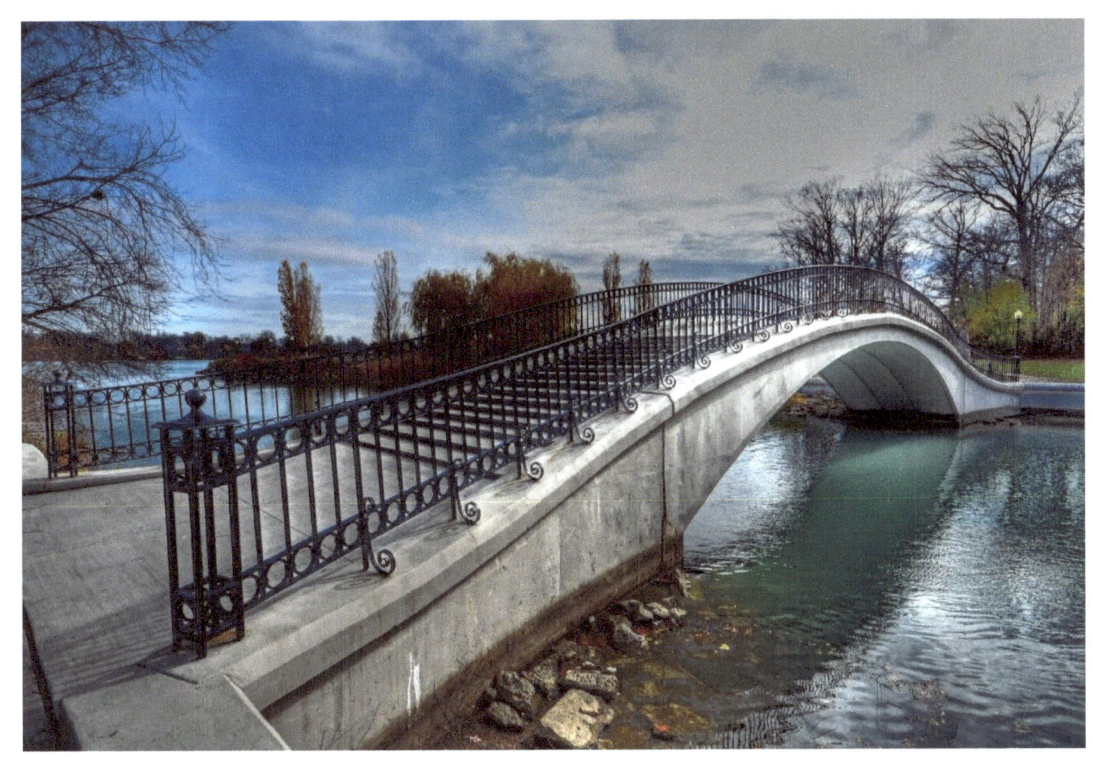

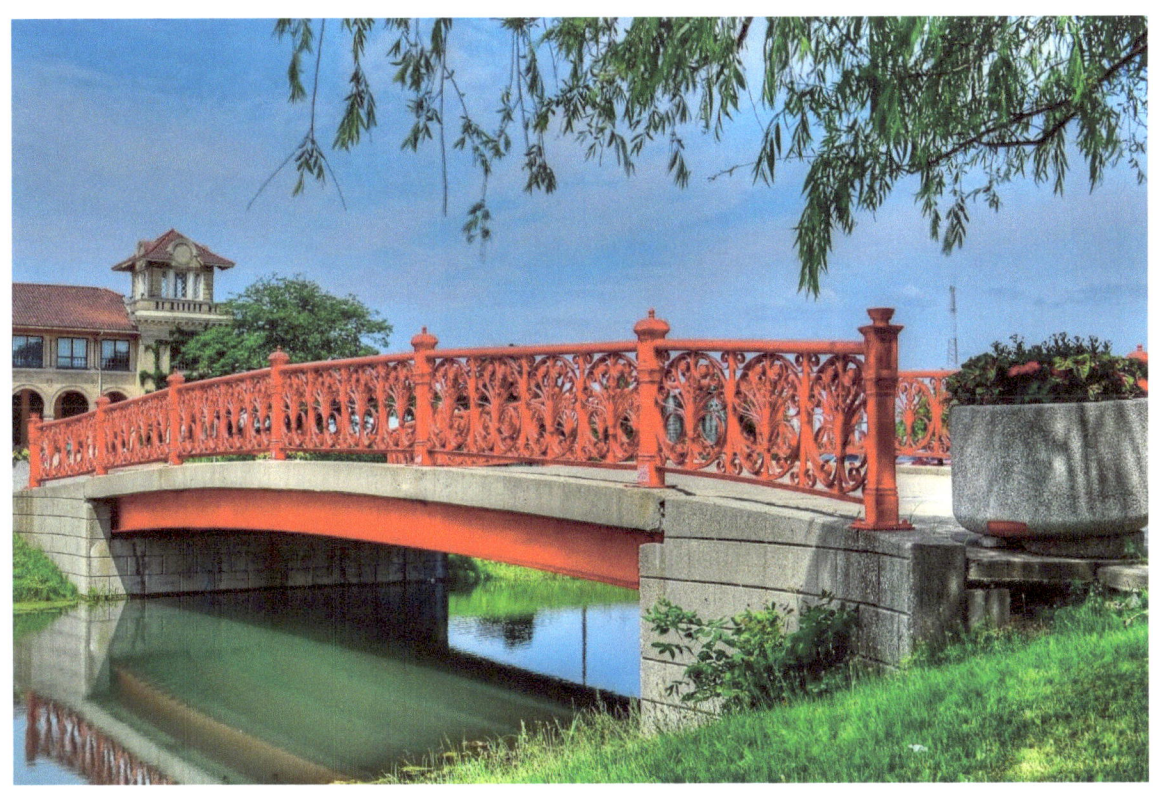

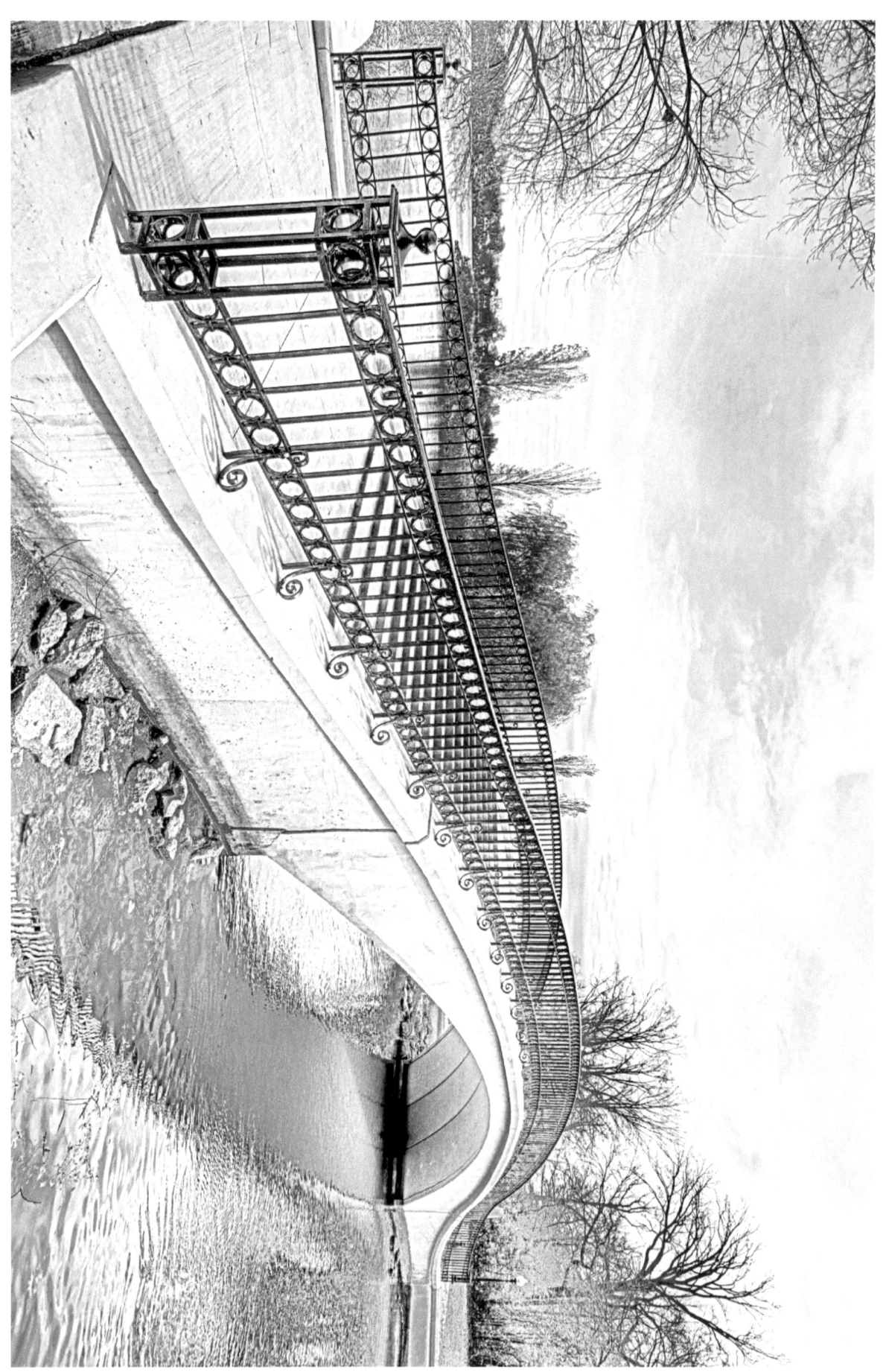

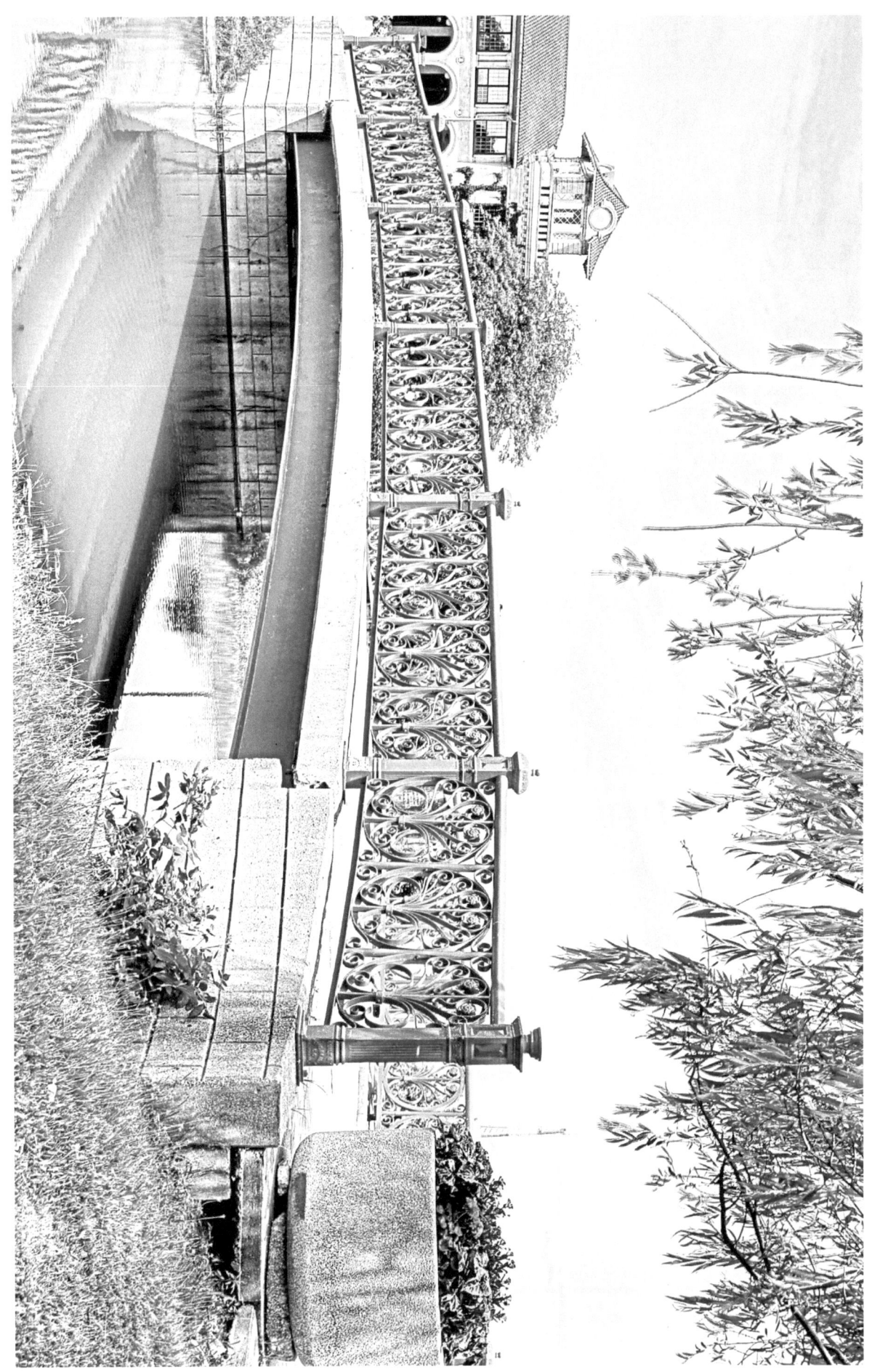

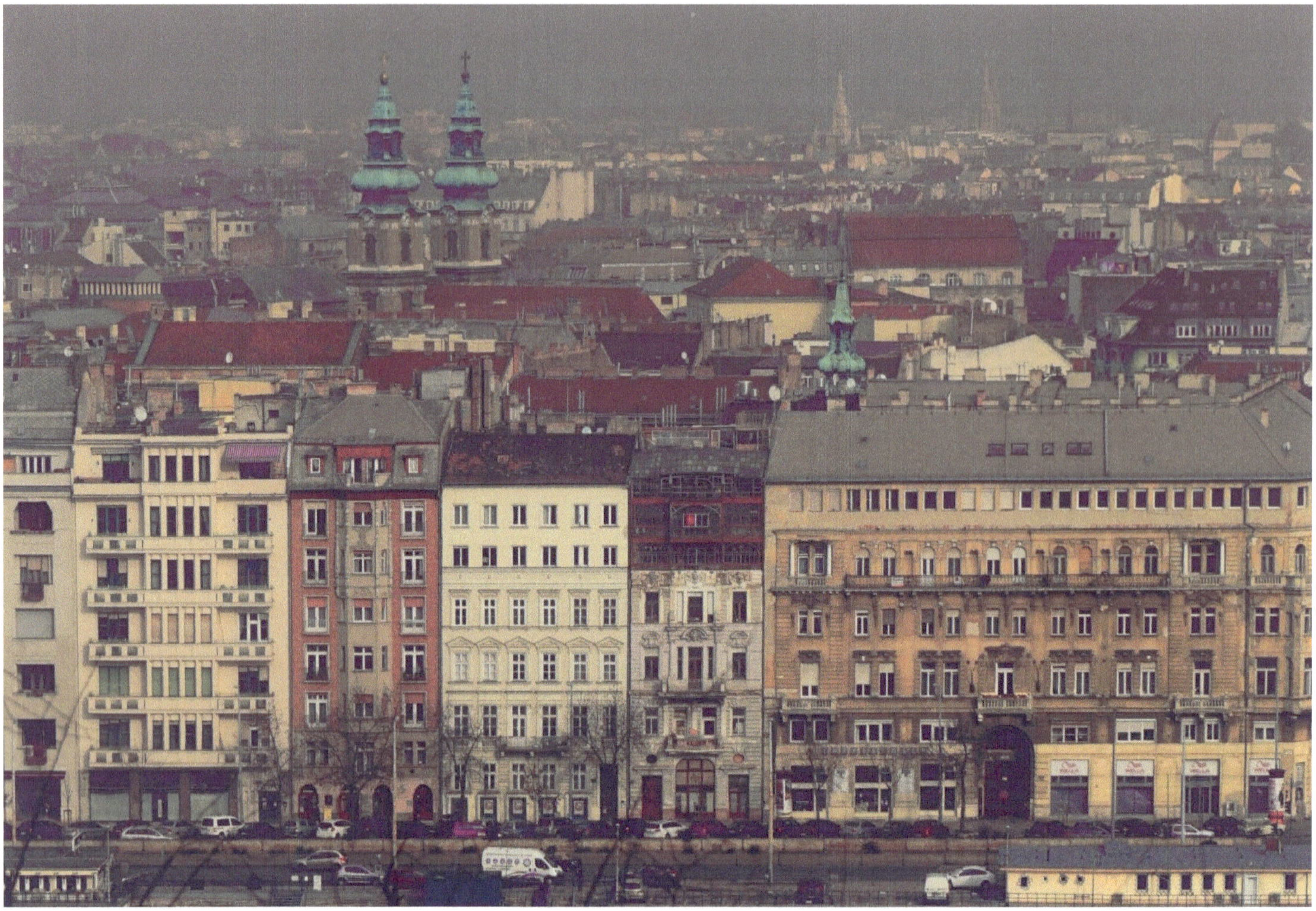

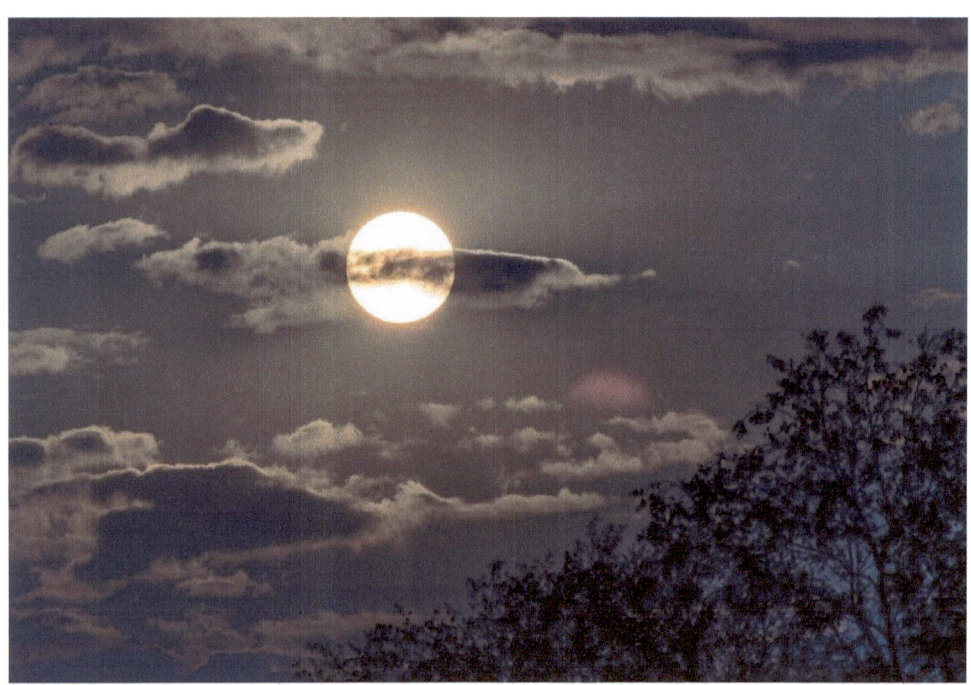

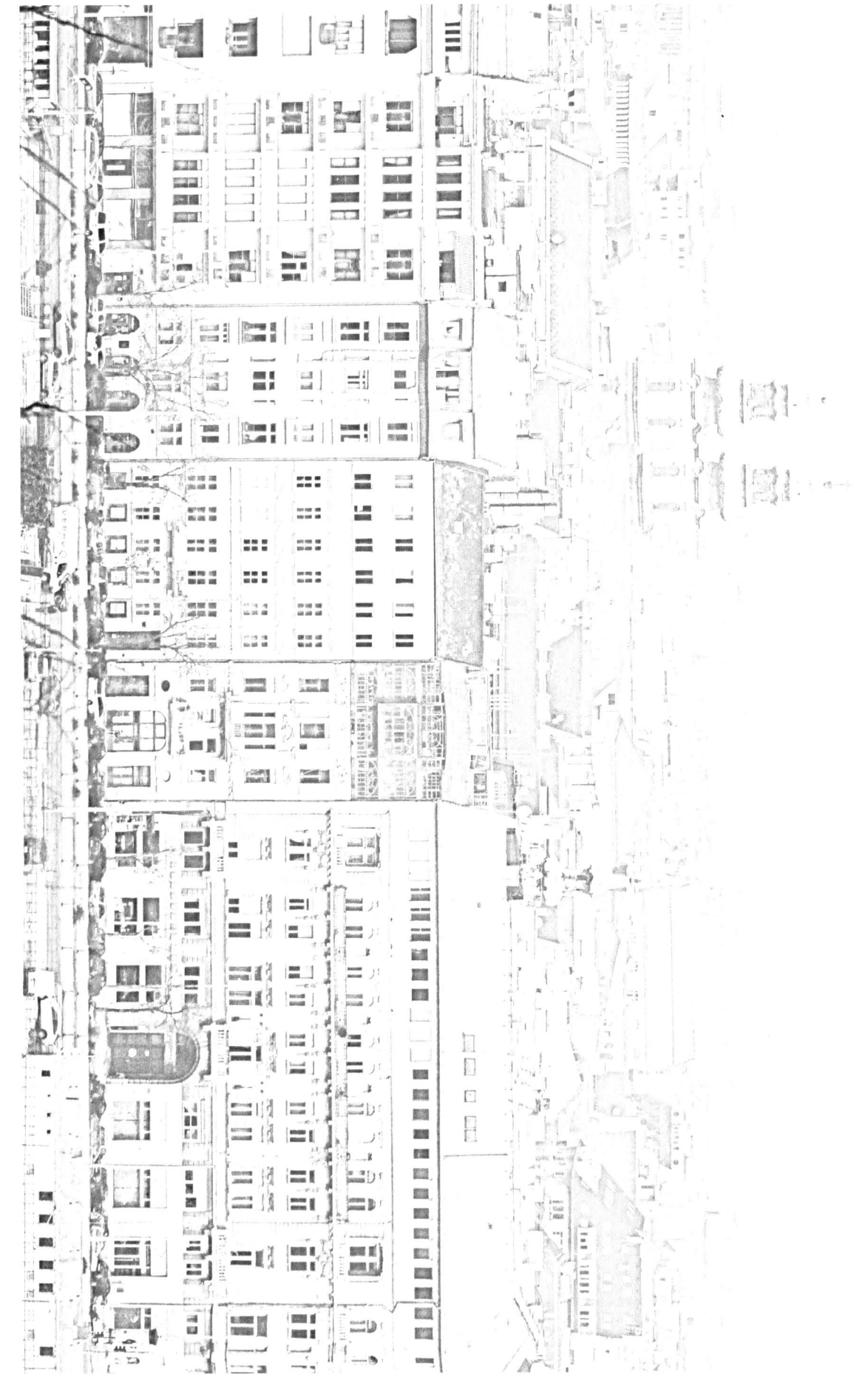

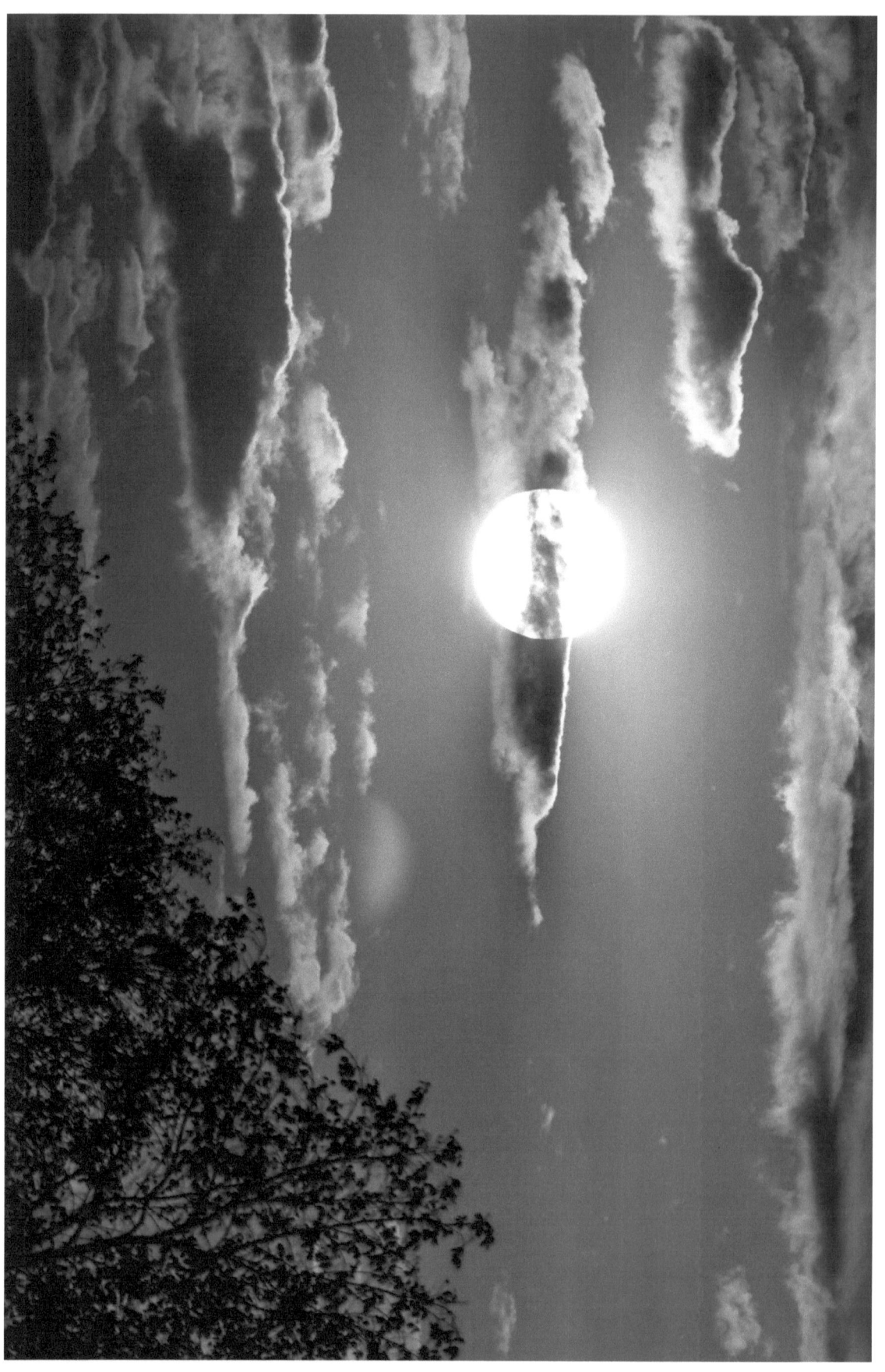

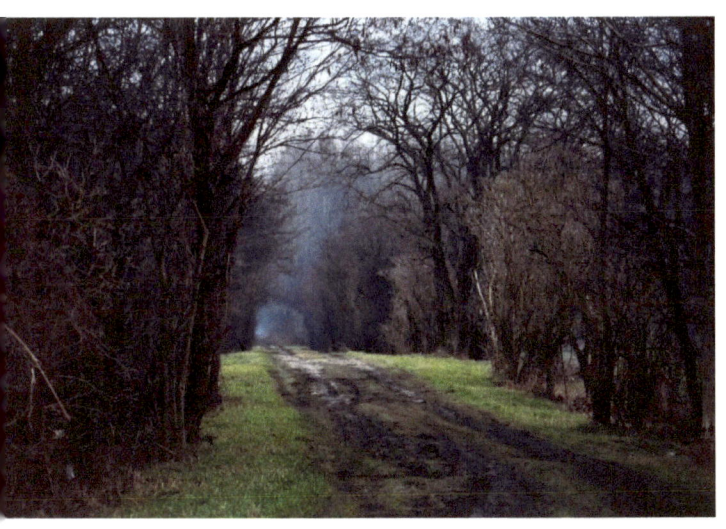

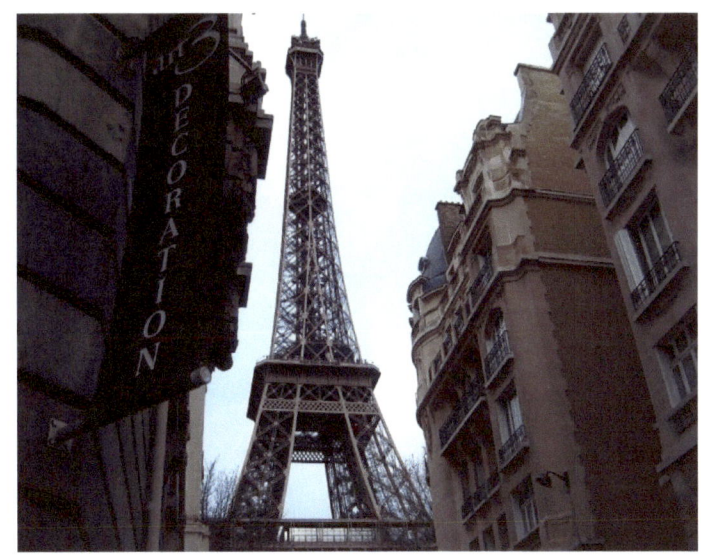

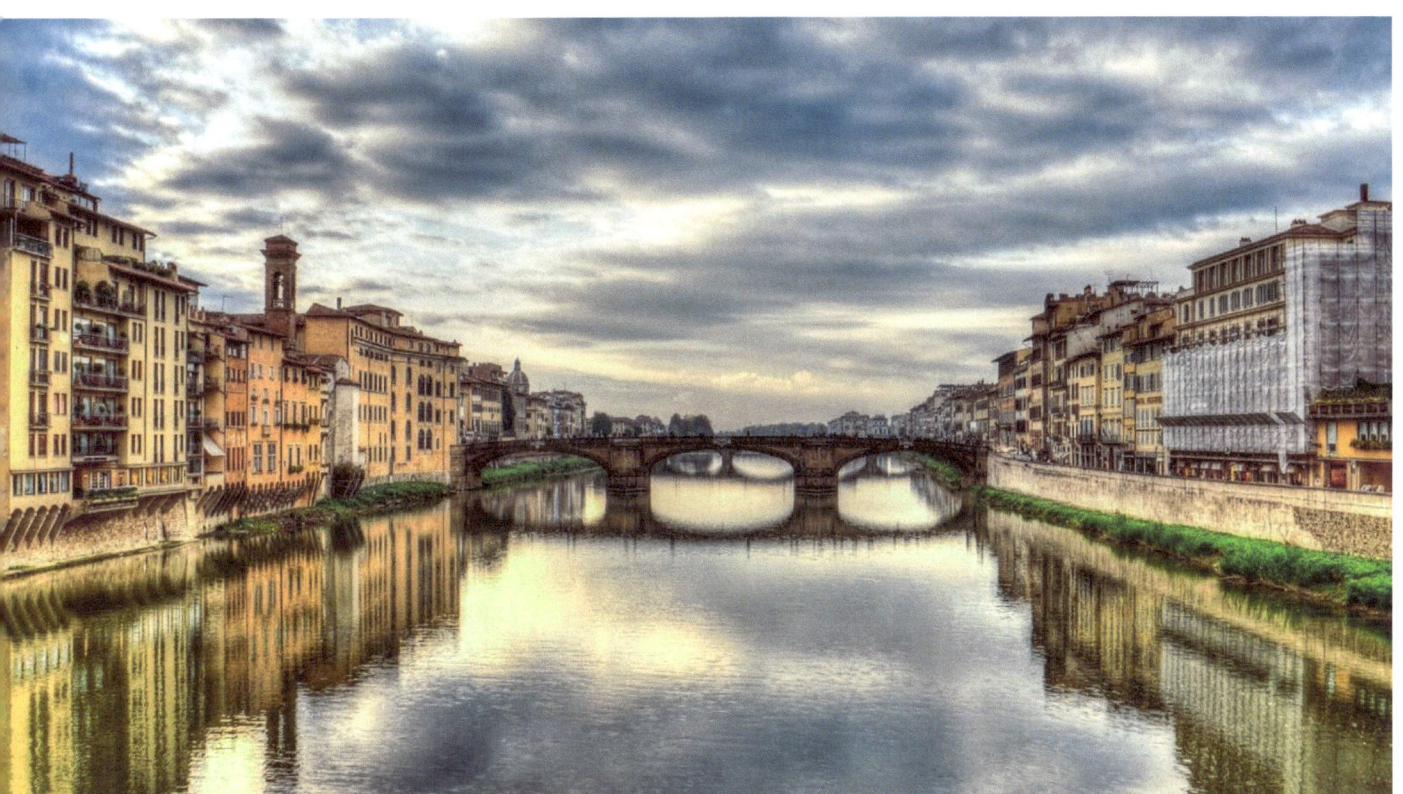

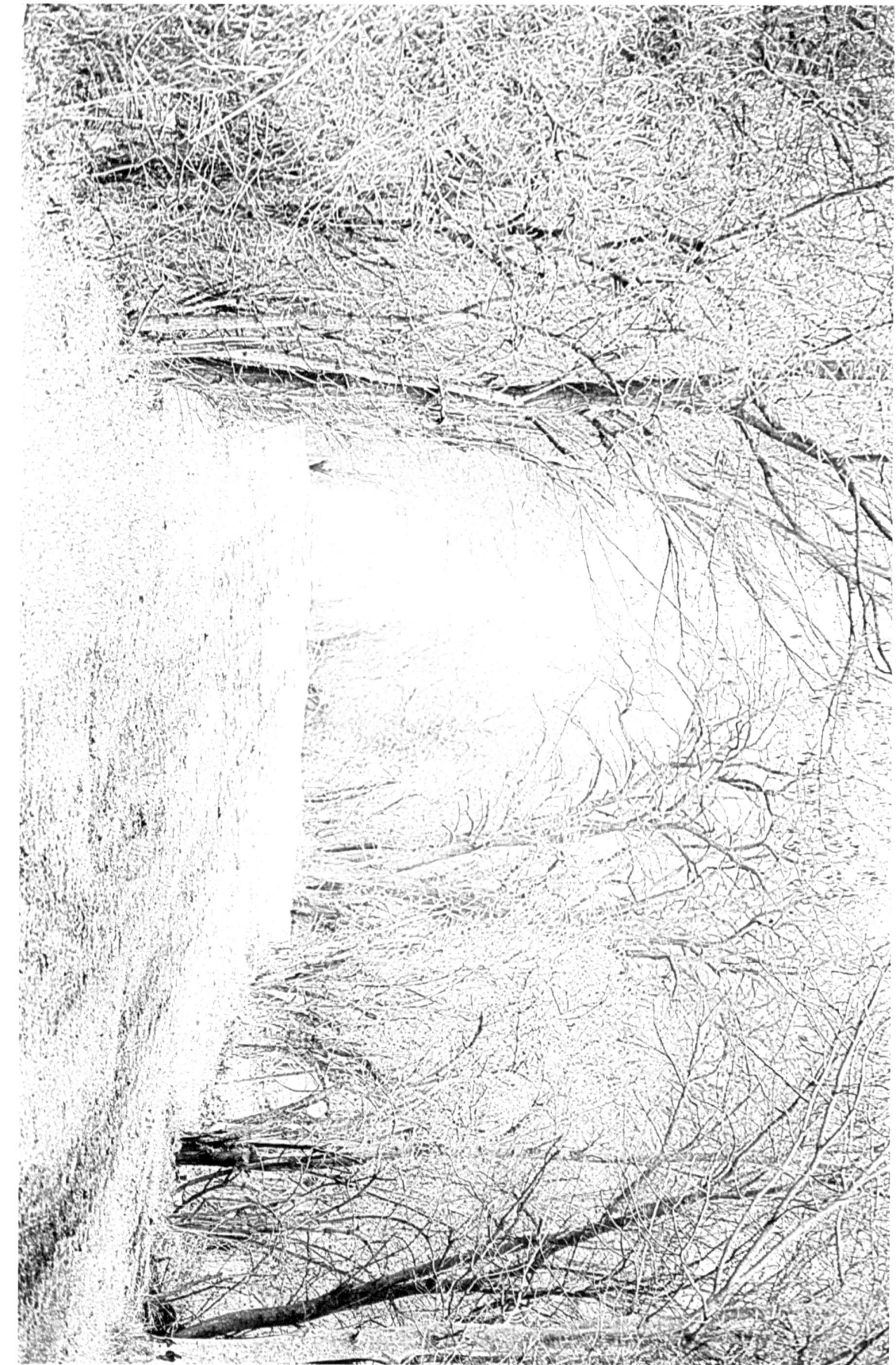

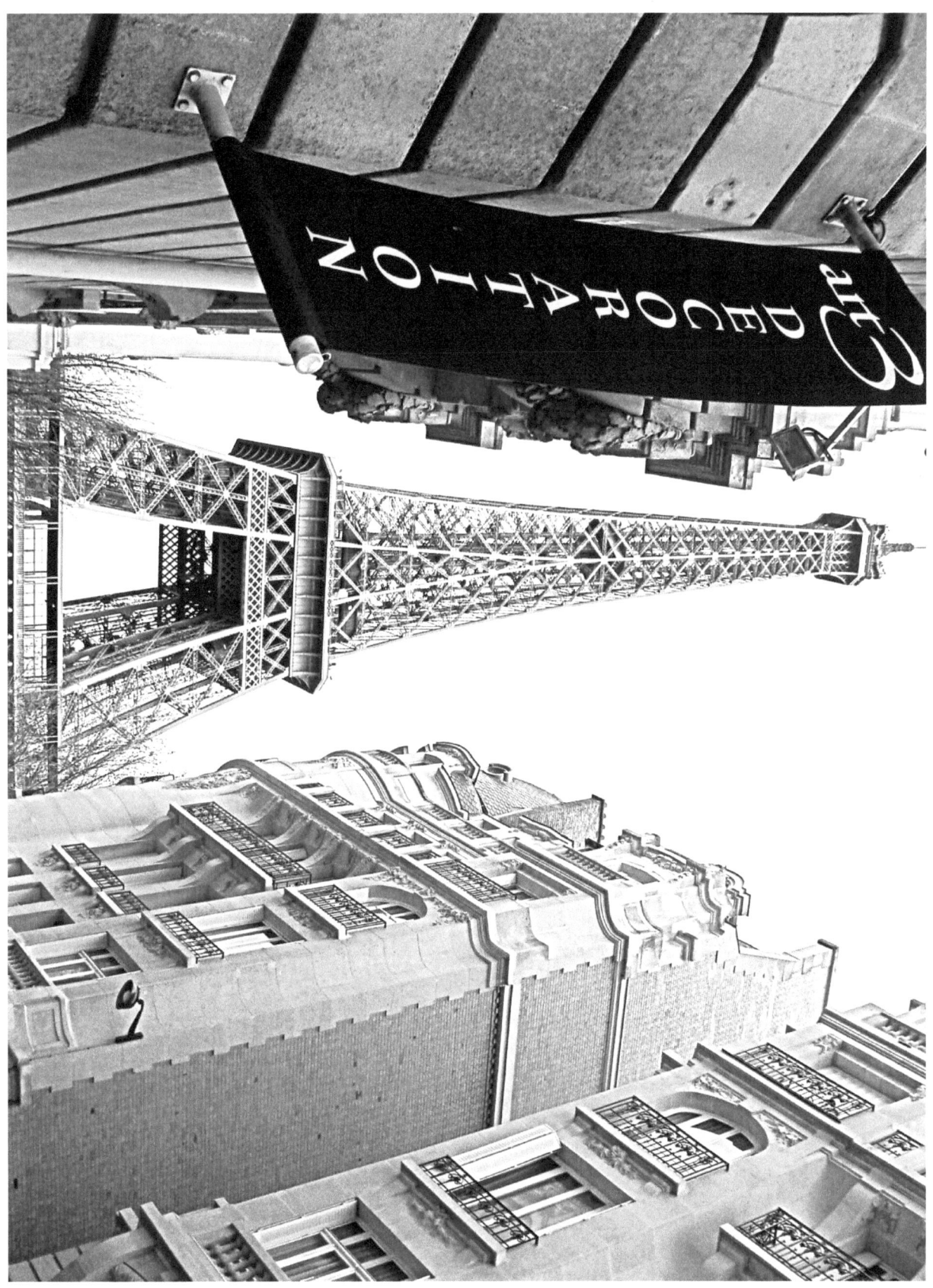

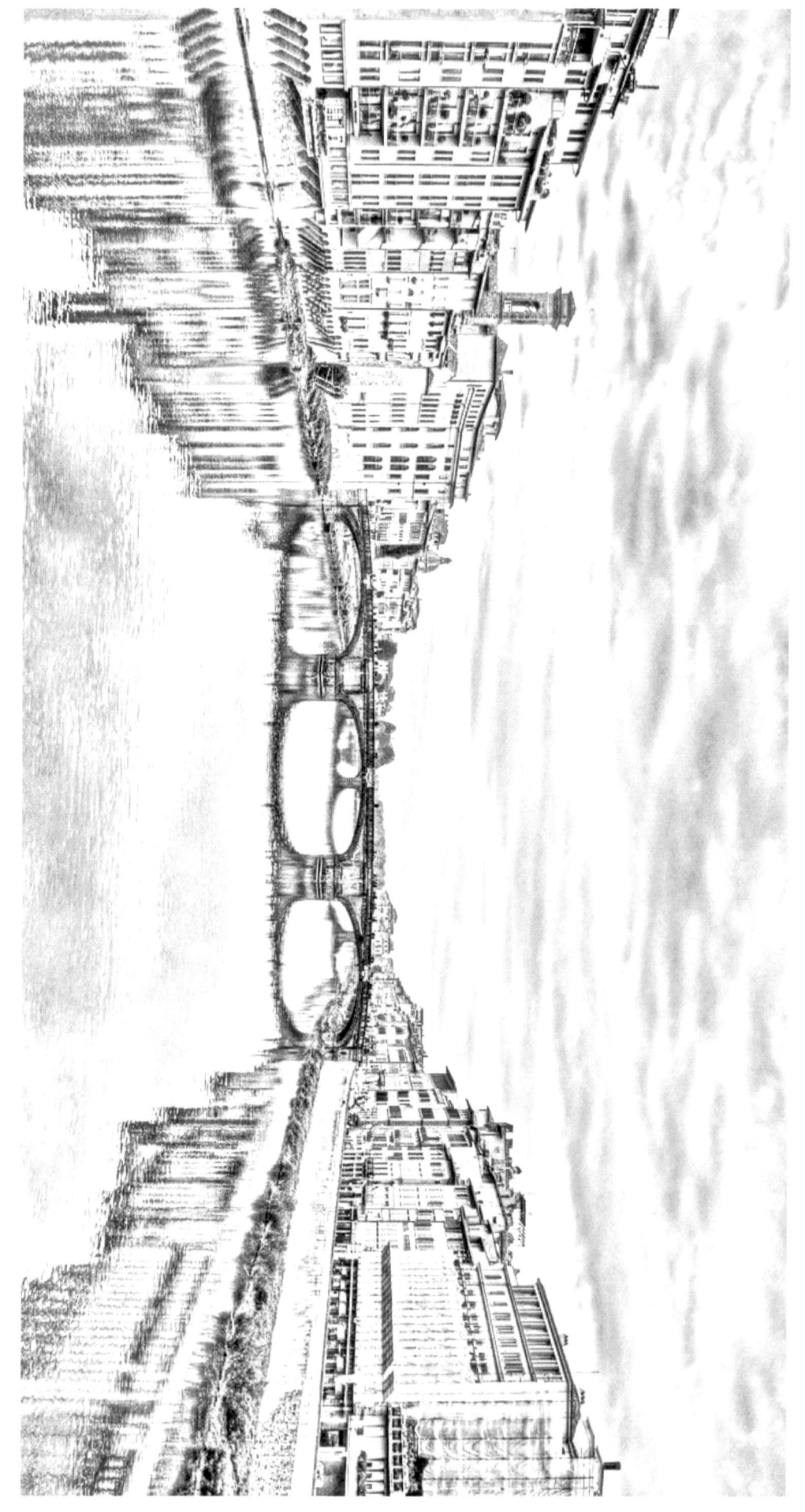

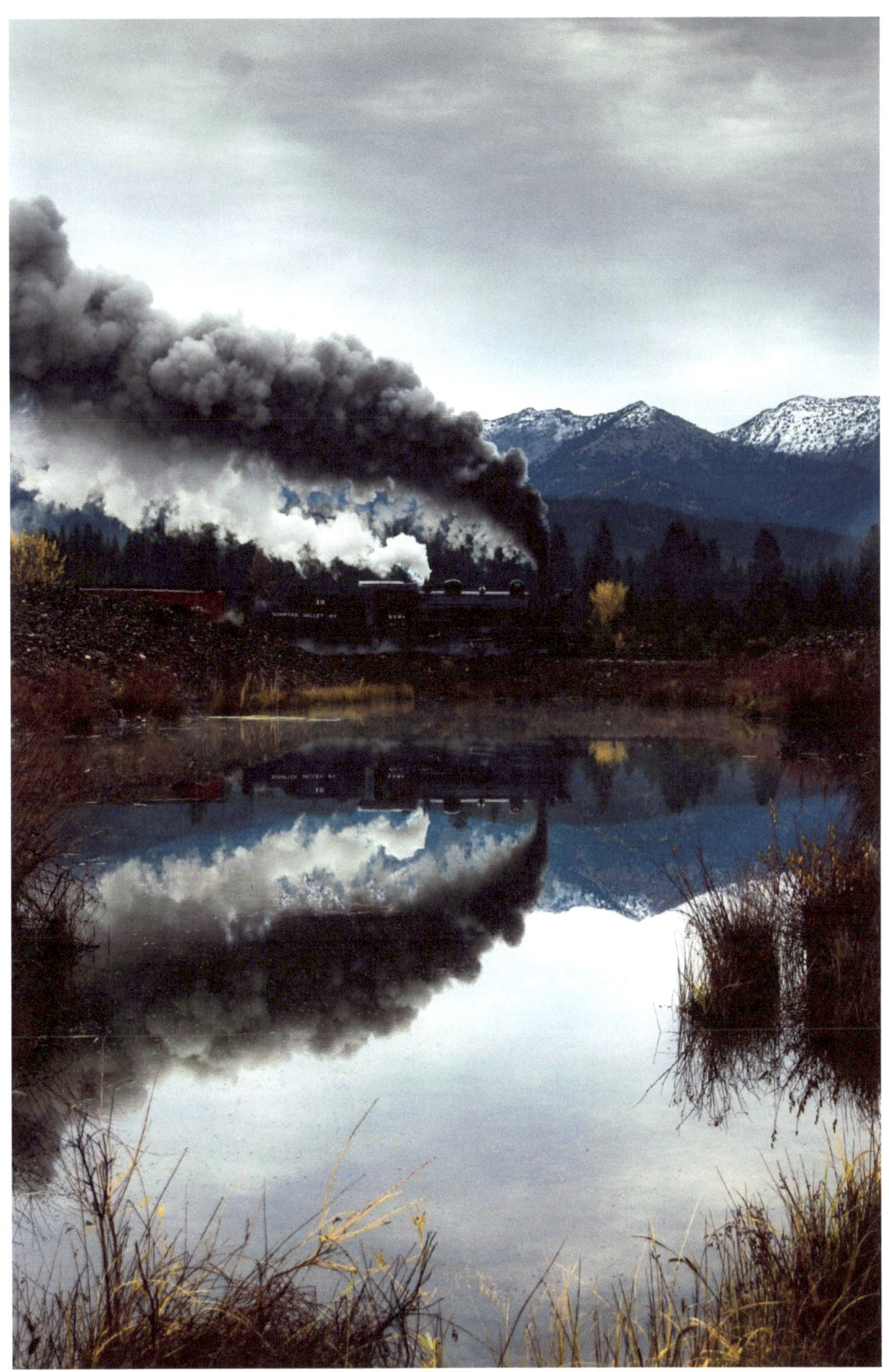

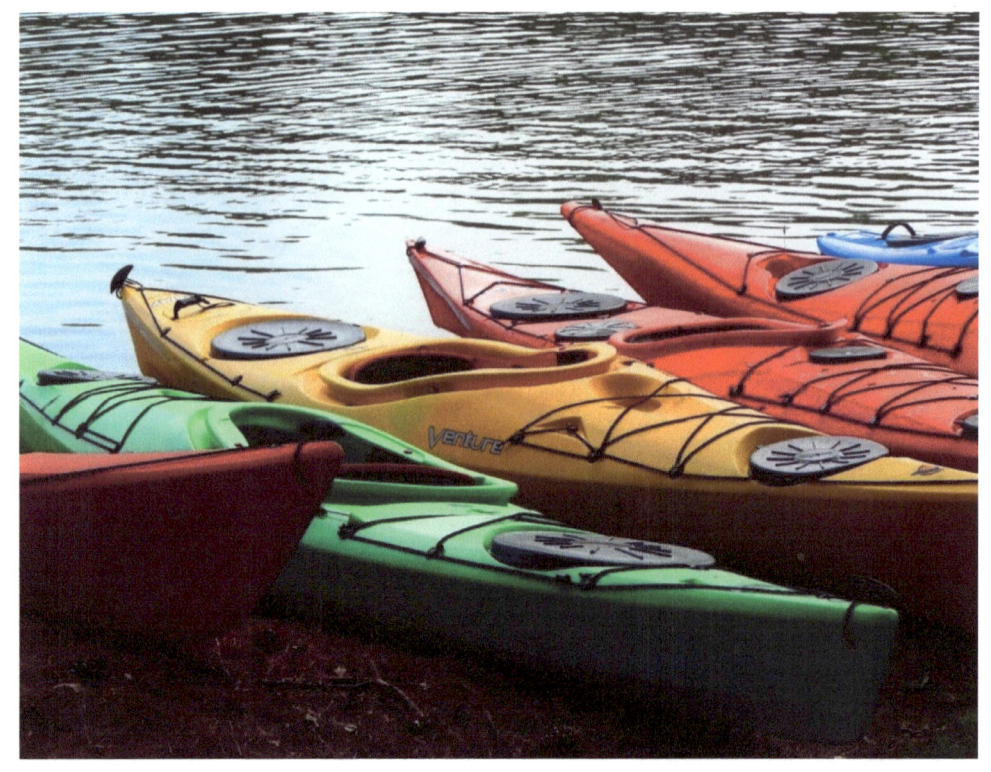

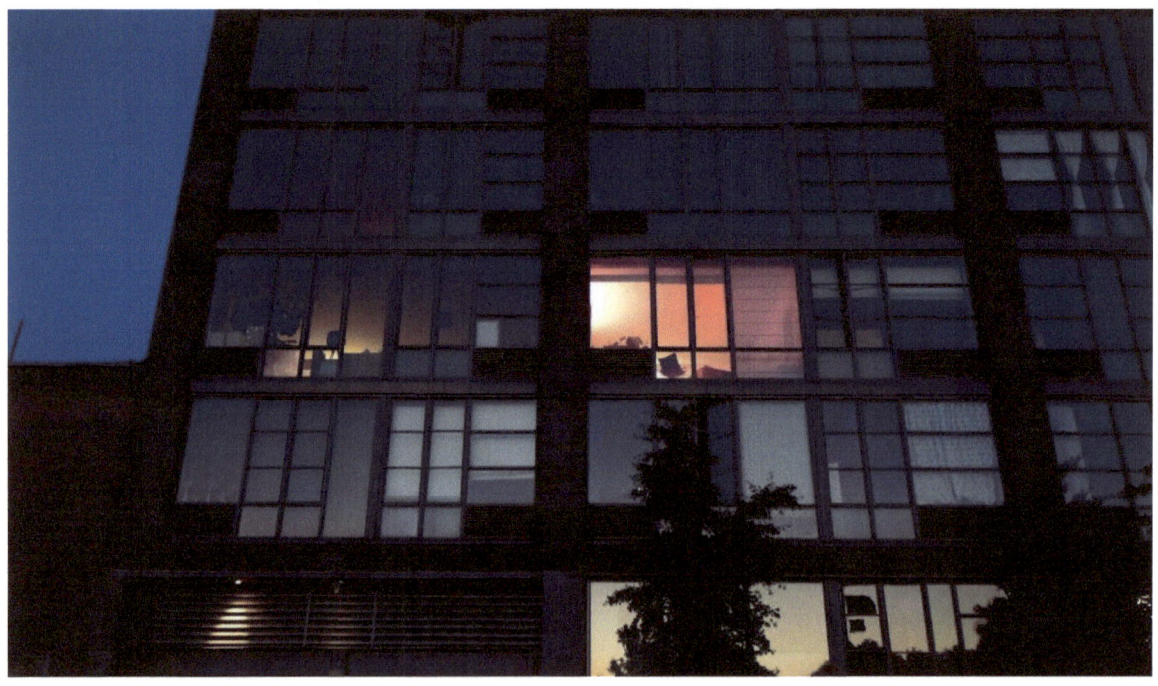

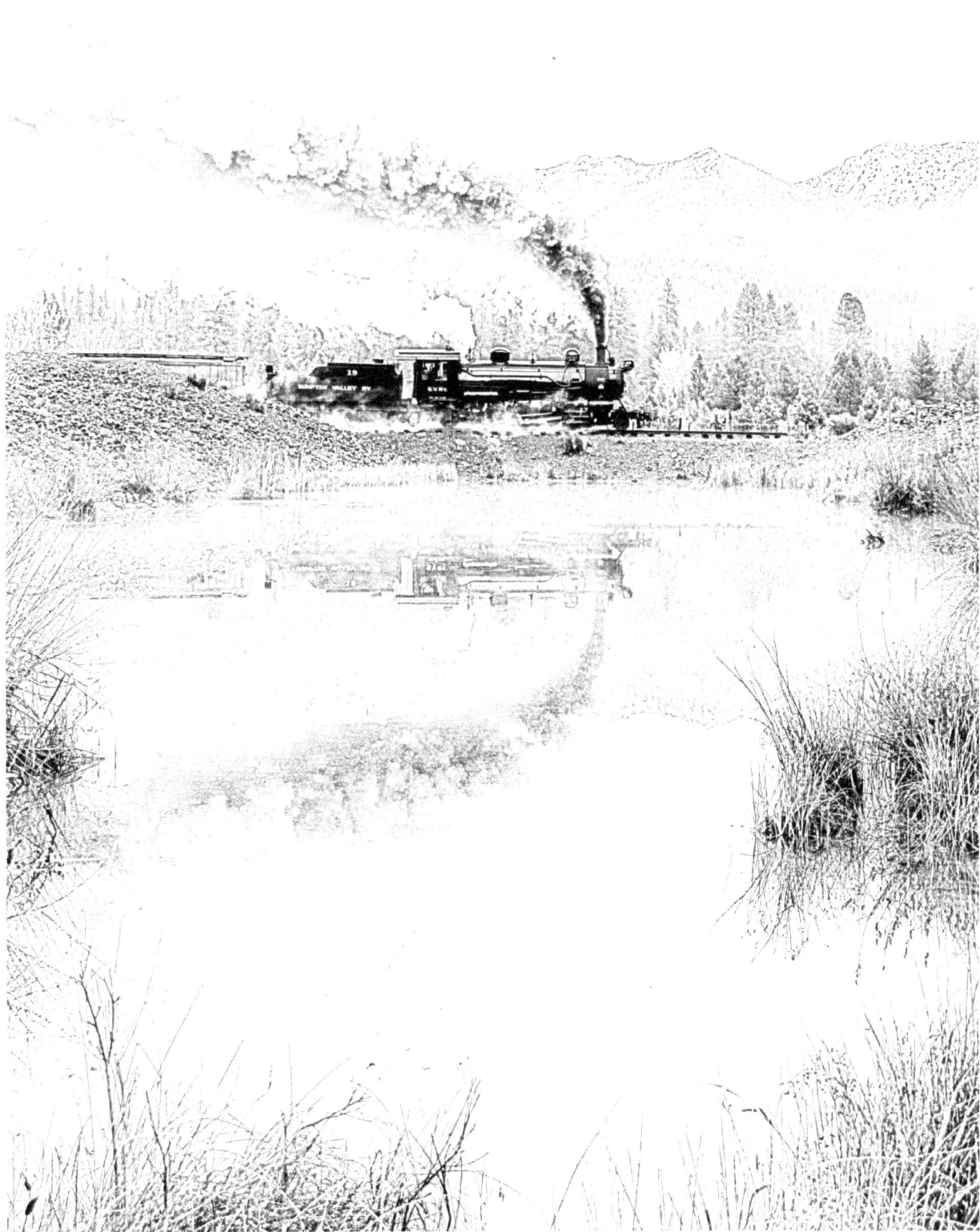

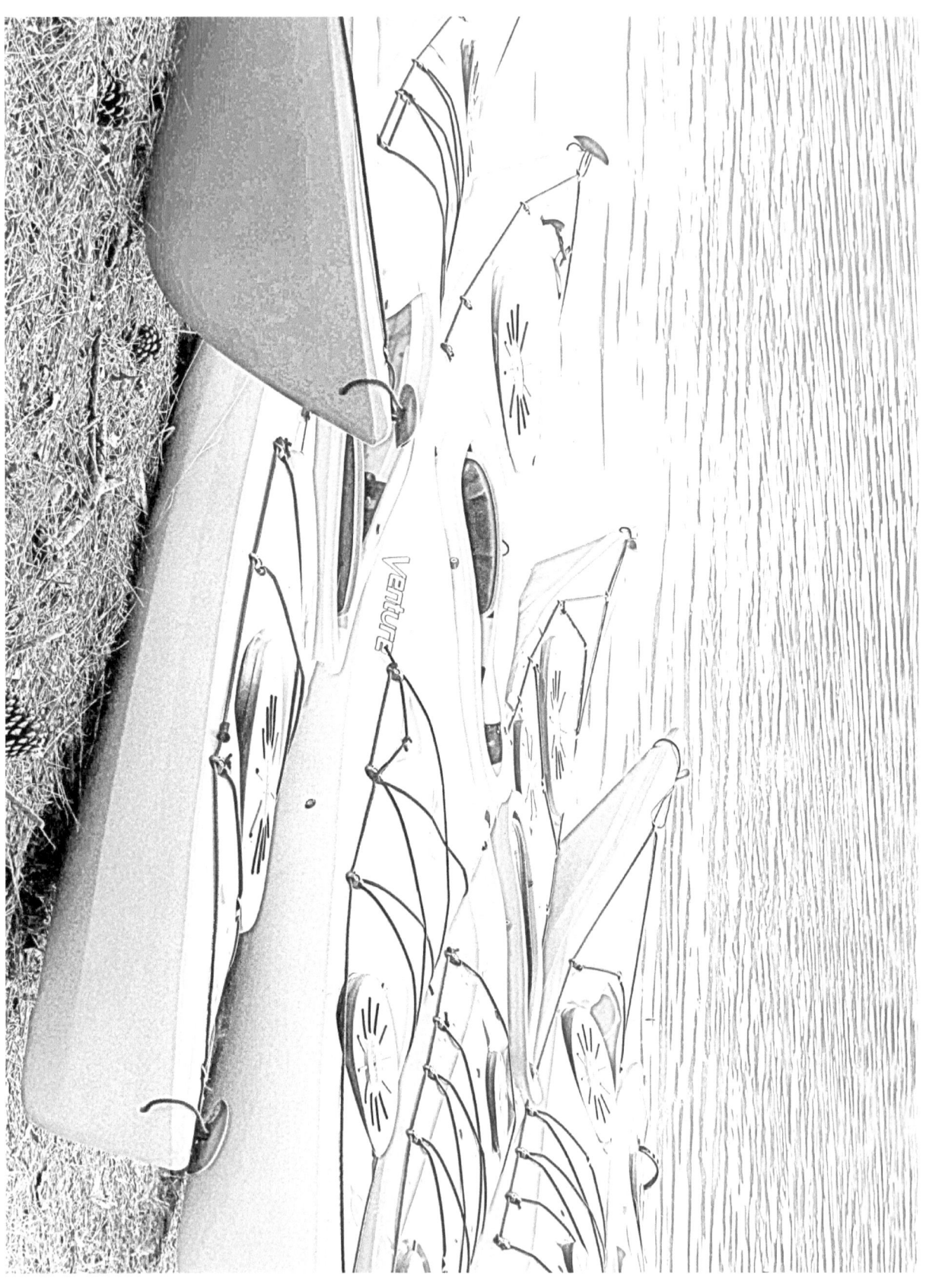

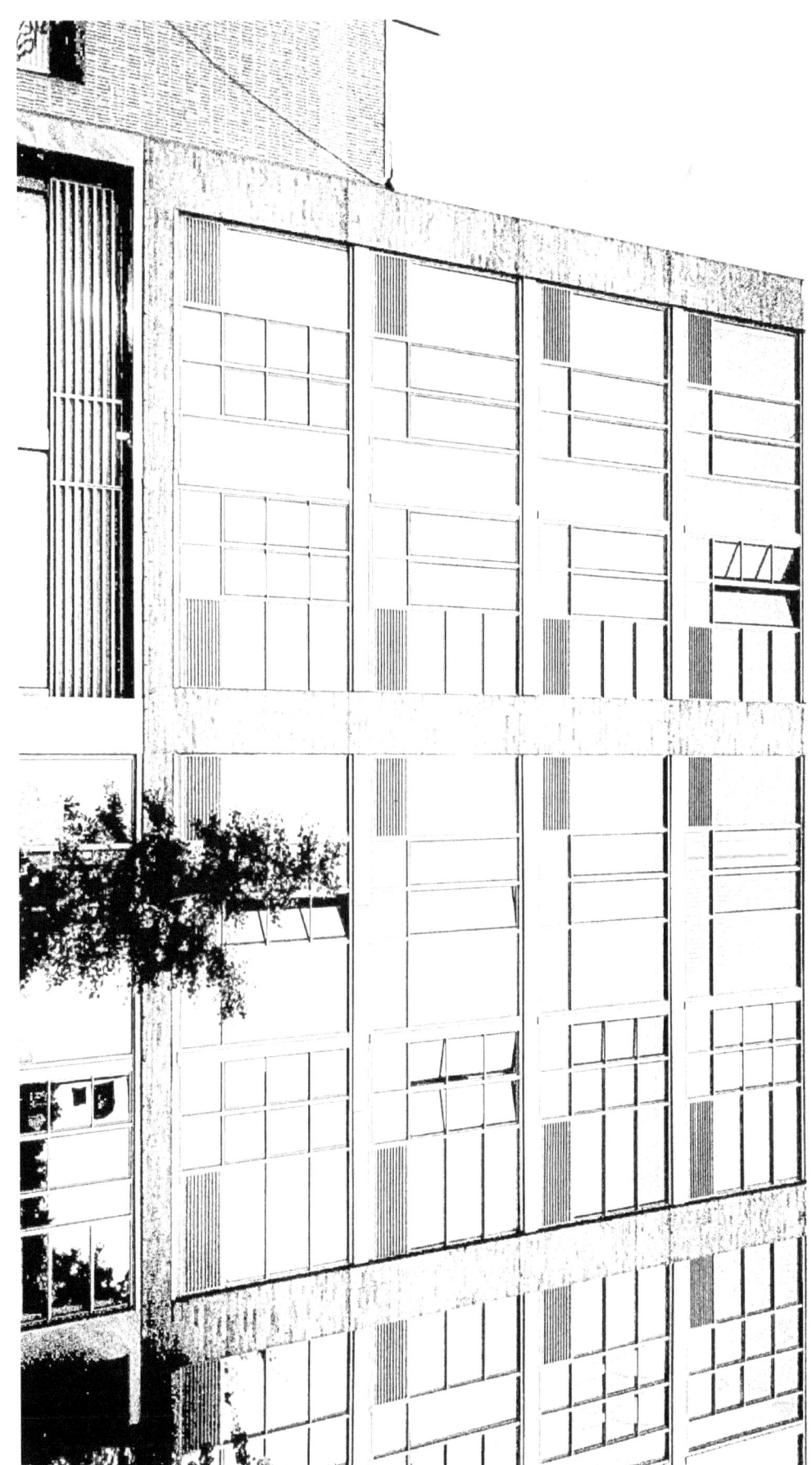

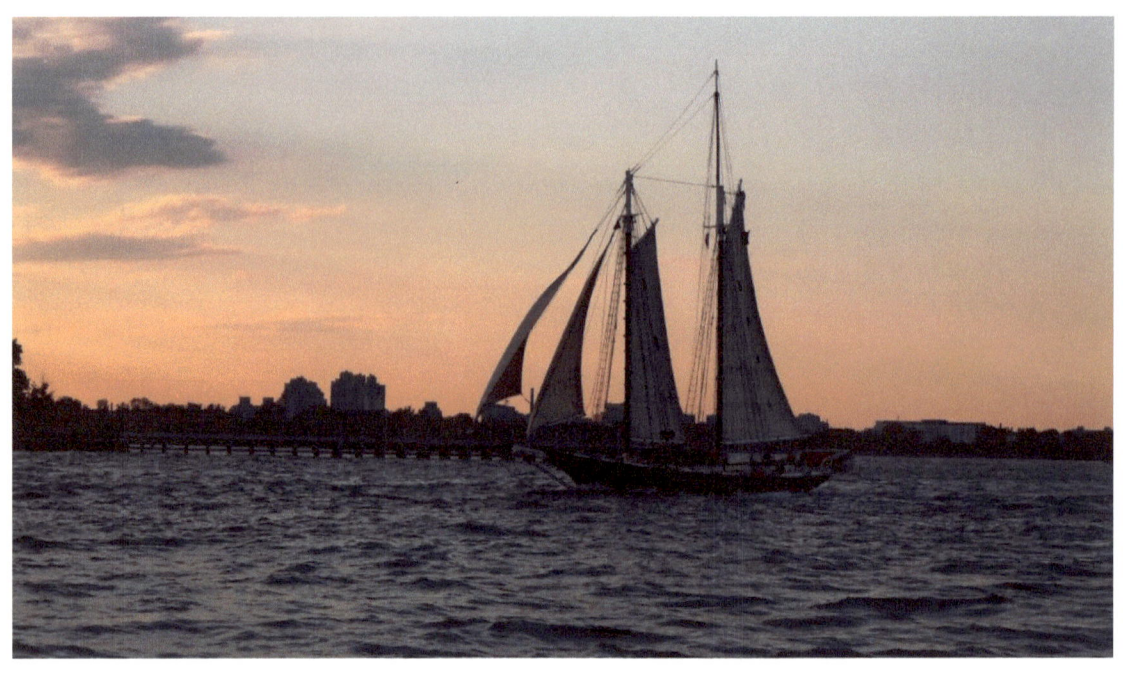

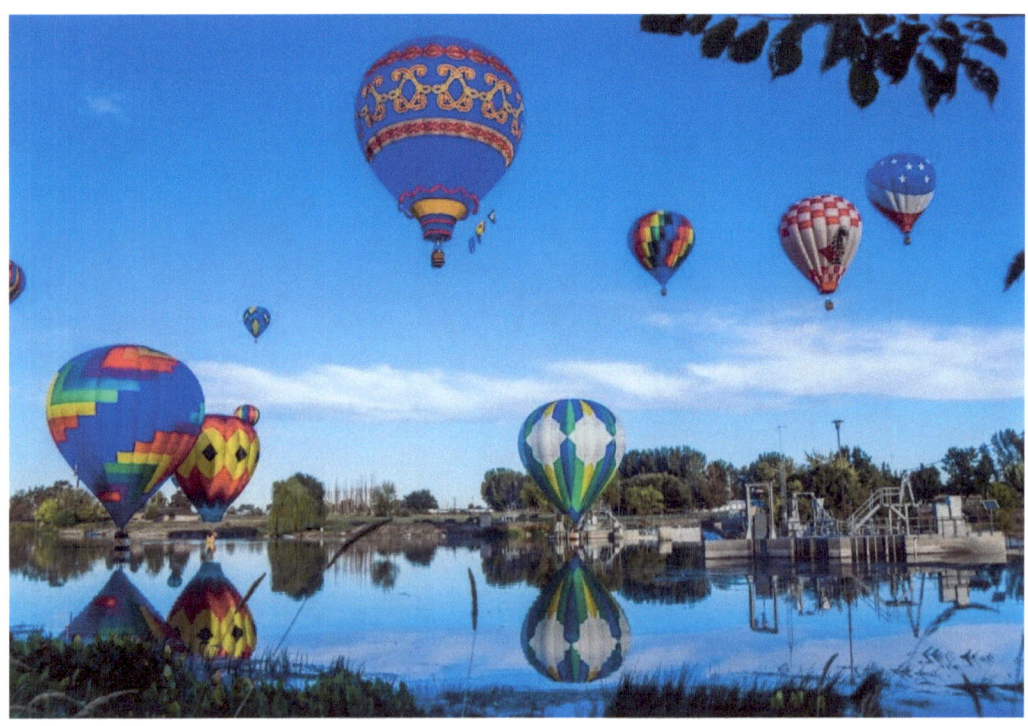

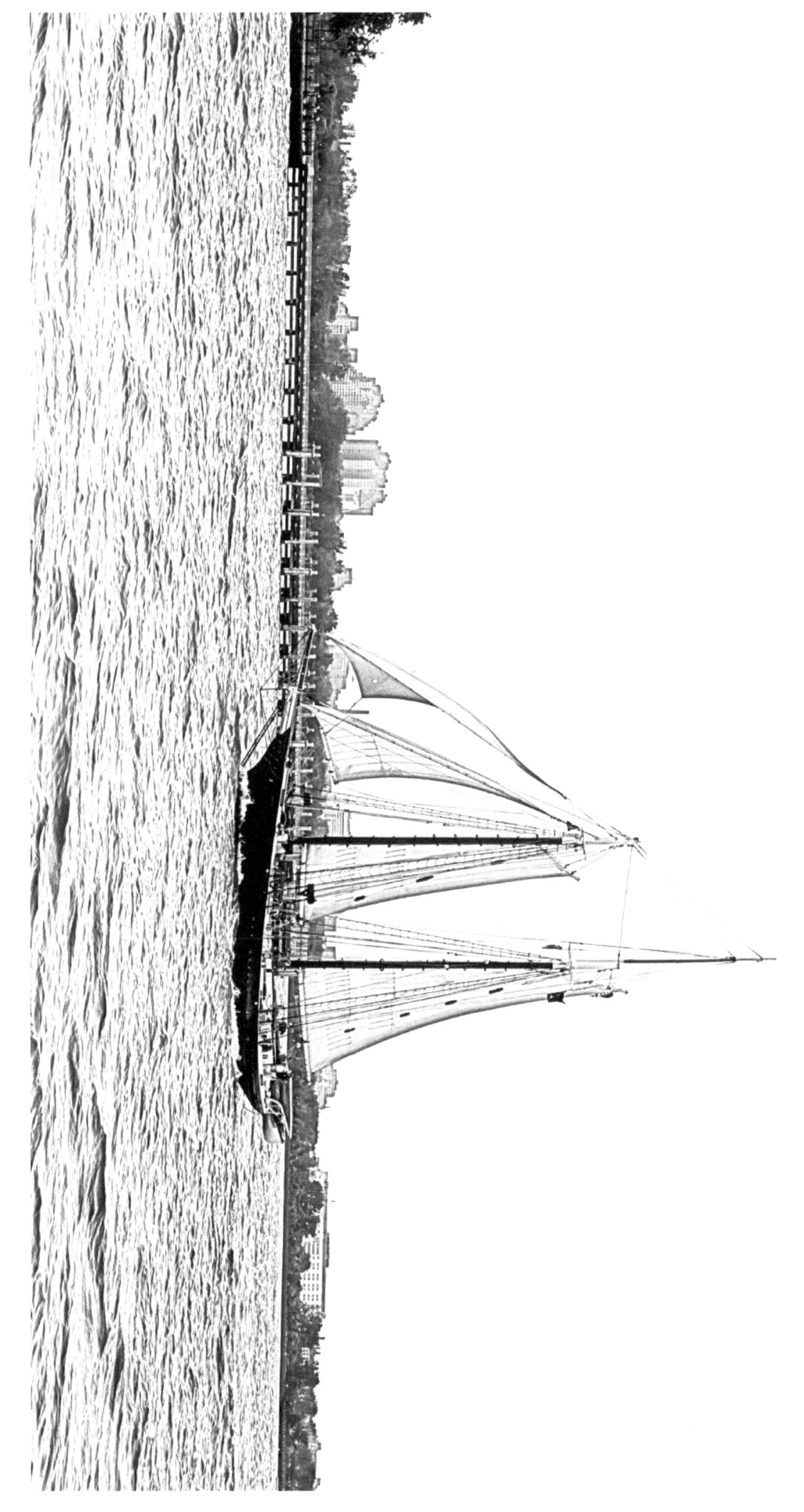

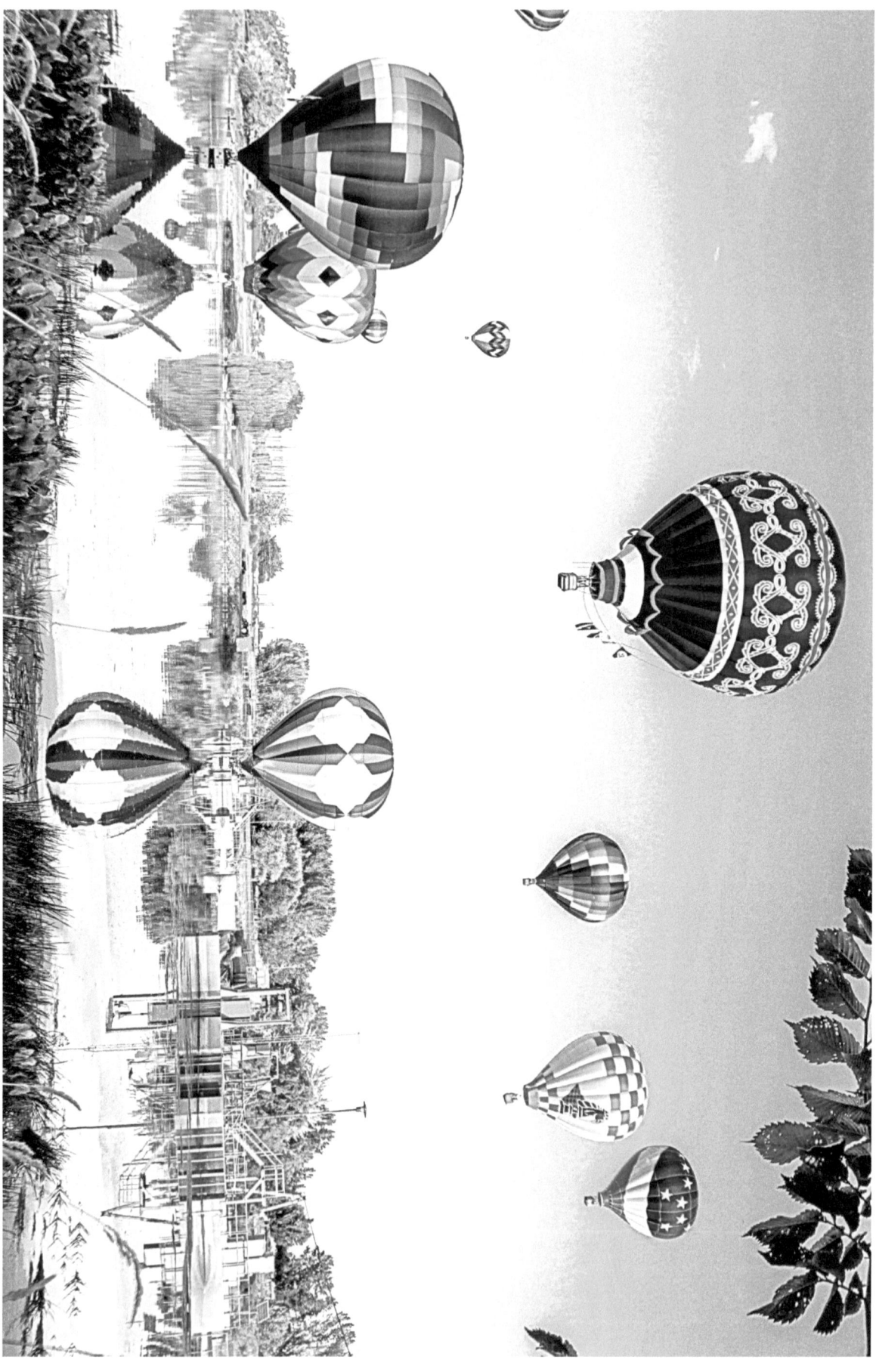

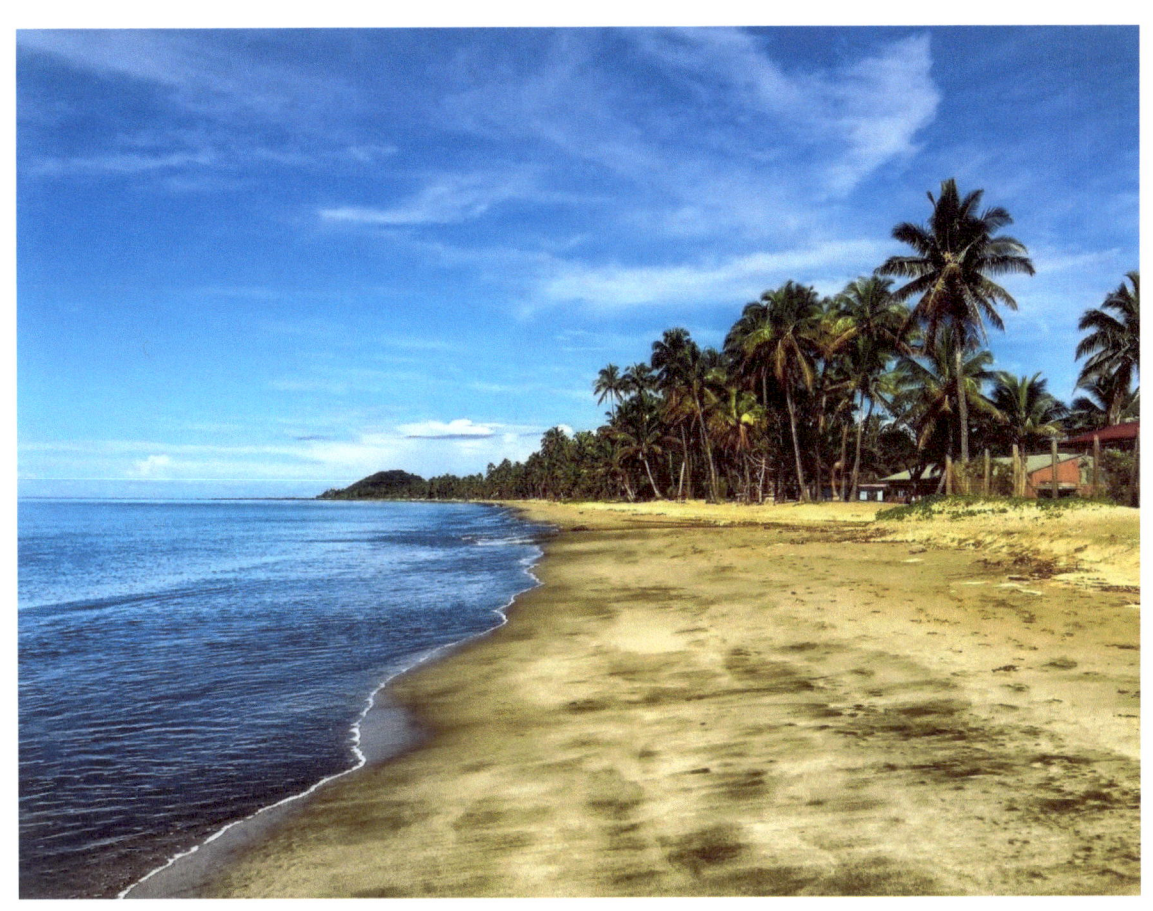

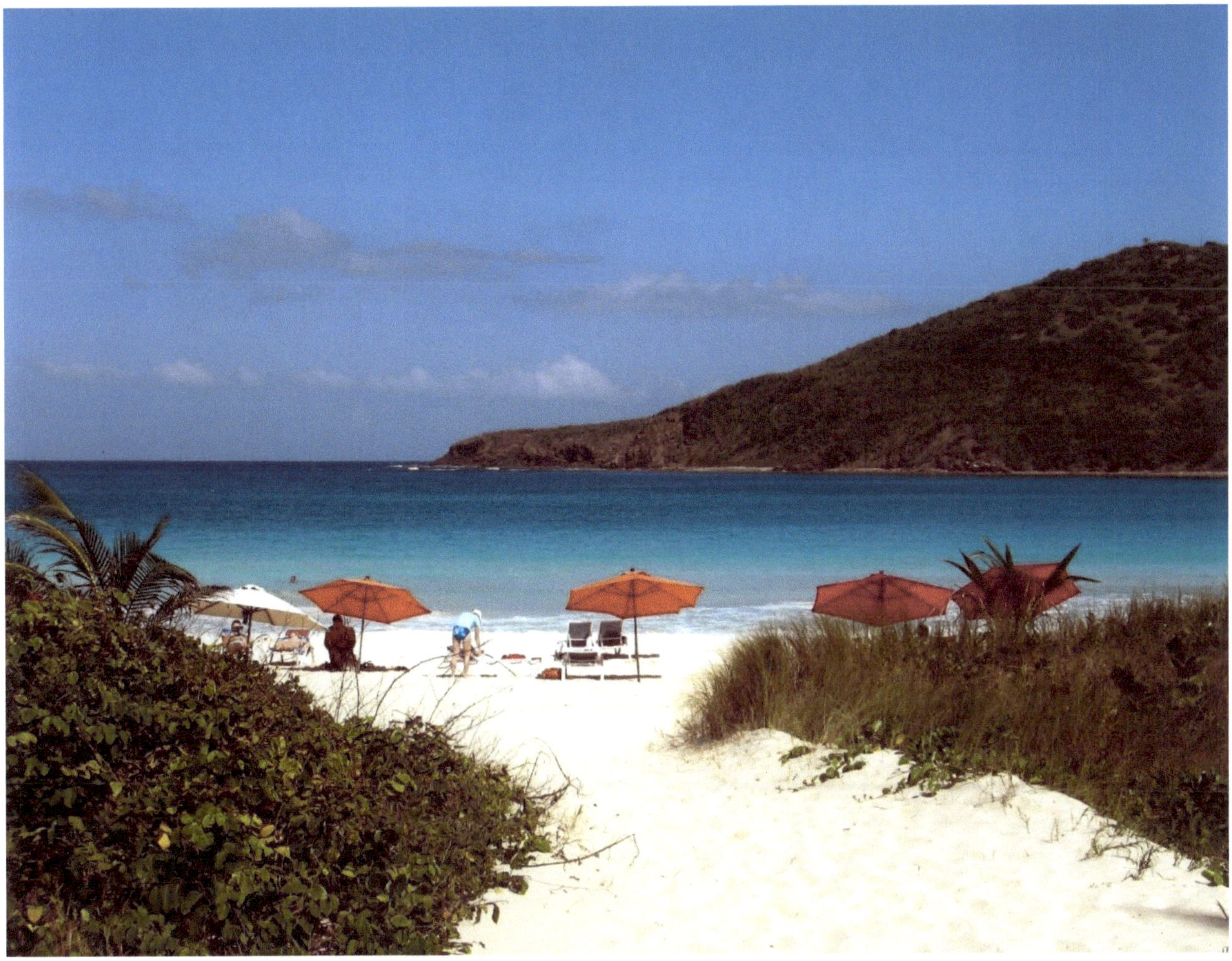

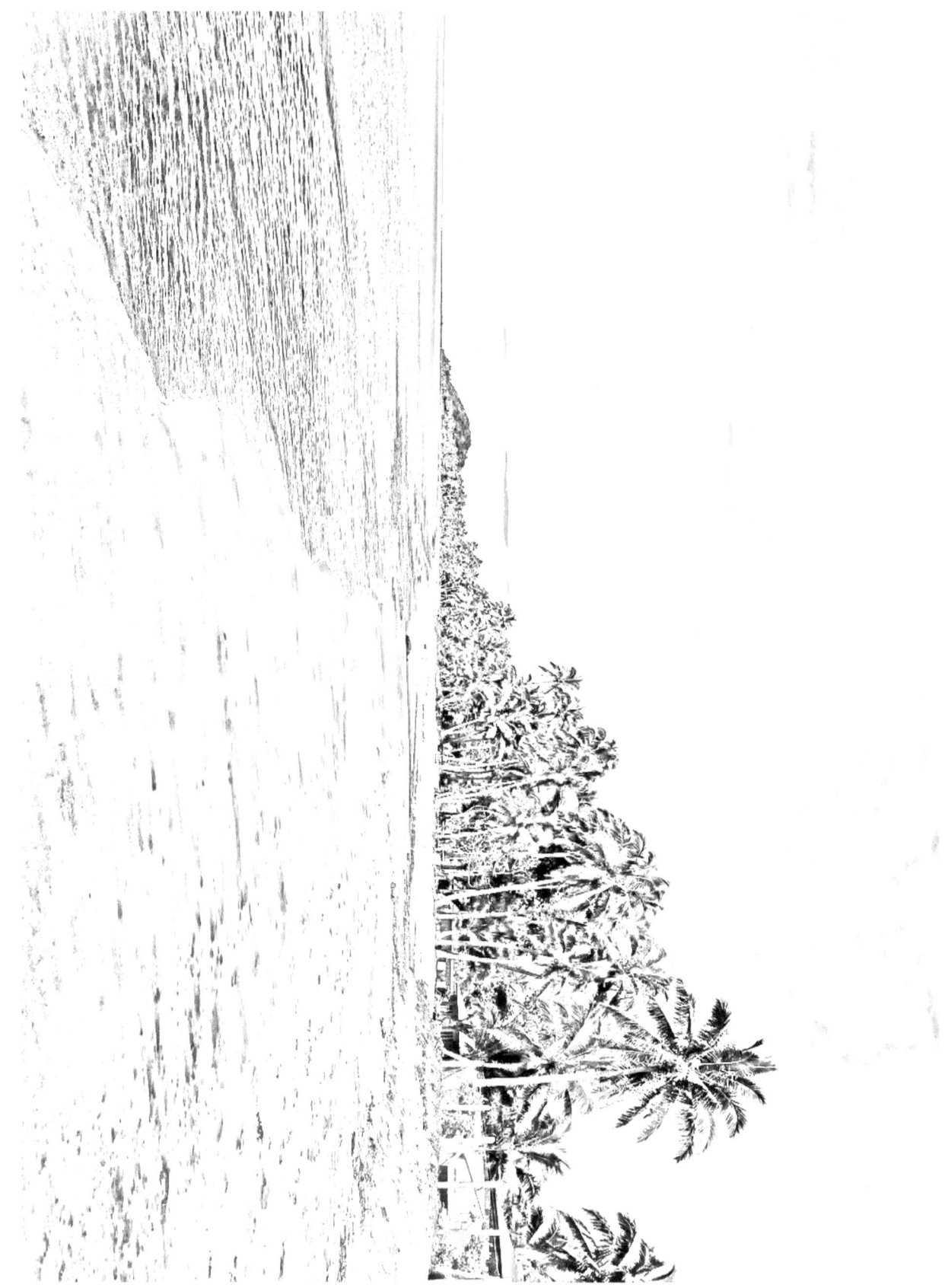

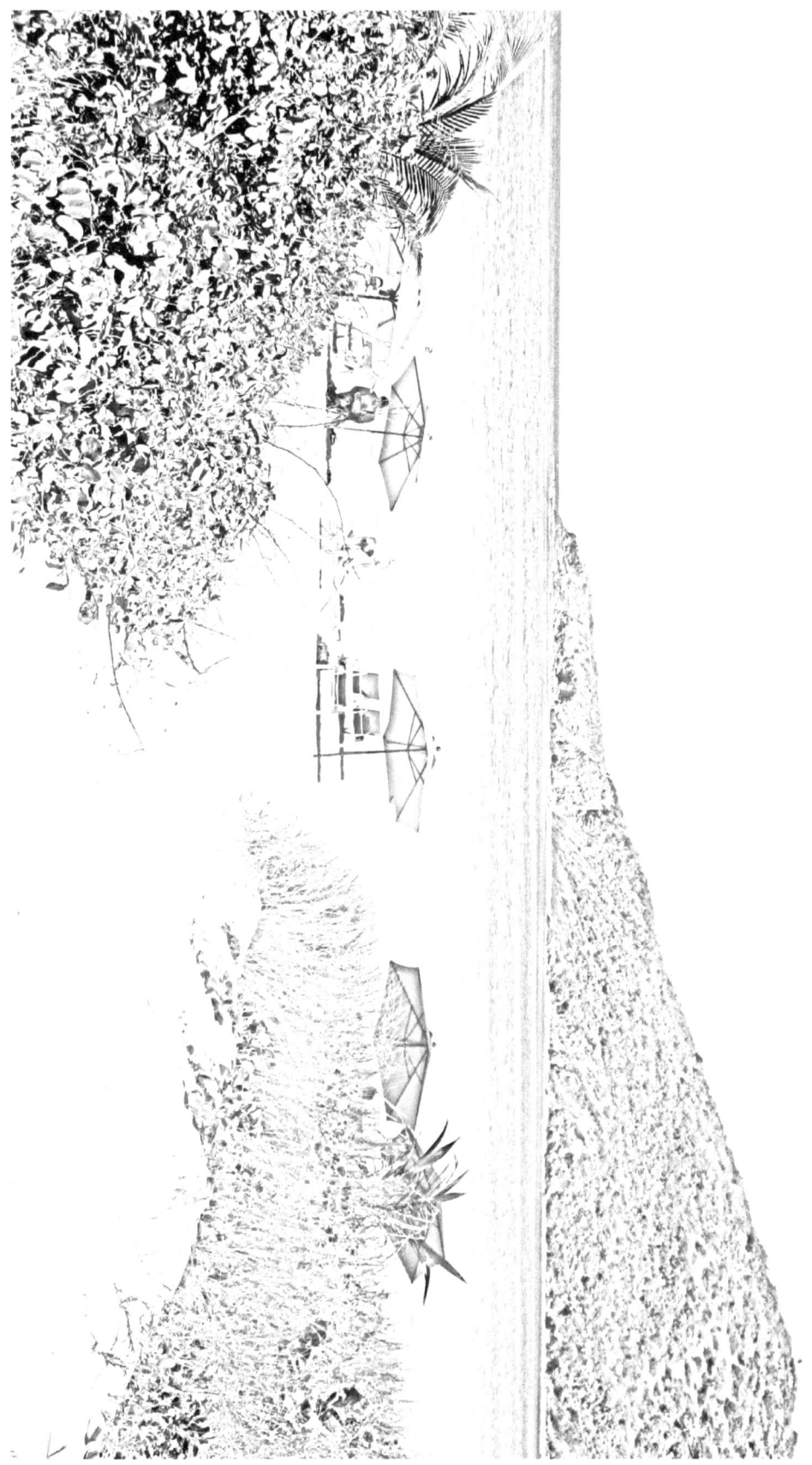